ENGLISH WORKSHOP

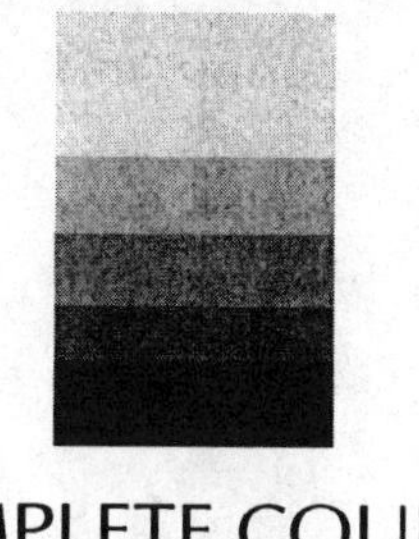

COMPLETE COURSE

TEACHER'S NOTES
WITH
ANSWER KEYS

HOLT, RINEHART AND WINSTON

Harcourt Brace & Company

Austin • New York • Orlando • Chicago • Atlanta
San Francisco • Boston • Dallas • Toronto • London

ACKNOWLEDGMENTS

We wish to thank the following teachers who reviewed materials for *English Workshop*, either in manuscript or in field tests.

Sandra Beane
Beachwood High School
Beachwood, OH 44122

Paula L'Homme
West Orange High School
Winter Garden, FL 34787

Jo O'Brien
Troy High School
Troy, MI 48098

Karen Reichert
Uniontown High School
Uniontown, PA 15401

Dr. Ester Scott
Lincoln High School
Los Angeles, CA 90031

A NOTE TO THE TEACHER

The Teacher's Notes provides an overview of issues and concepts related to the teaching of English.

The Answer Key for the Pupil's Edition lists answers for Chapters One through Twenty-four. For the teacher's convenience, a suggested rubric is included for each form of writing presented in "Aims for Writing," Chapters Four through Seven.

The Answer Key for the Assessment Booklet gives both Diagnostic Test and Posttest answers for Chapters Ten through Twenty-four. Each twenty-question test has a total point value of 100 and may be scored individually.

7 8 9 10 095 05 04 03 02

CONTENTS

1866

TEACHER'S NOTES

THE AIMS AND MODES OF WRITING

Writing accomplishes something. It gets politicians elected (speeches and commercials) and workers promoted (job evaluations). It soothes pain (a diary) and causes chills (a horror novel). When students see what written language can do *for them*, learning to write becomes not just a school lesson but a life lesson.

Four Basic Aims

To express oneself, to create literature, to inform, to persuade—these four writing purposes, or aims, structure the writing lessons in *English Workshop*.

Expressive Writing. Expressive writing voices the writer's thoughts, feelings, or beliefs. The writing may be private, as in diaries, or public, as in personal essays or statements of faith. The emphasis is on the writer, and the approach is frankly subjective—though a specific piece of writing (relating an experience, for instance) may present data and facts.

Creative Writing. Creative writing uses language inventively to stimulate the thoughts, feelings, and imaginations of readers. While all writing involves originality and imaginative thinking, the term *creative writing* highlights creation in literary forms: novels, plays, and poems, as well as jokes, movies, and popular songs. The emphasis is on imagination and on language itself.

Expository Writing. Expository writing informs or explains. It may also explore complex ideas. Exposition includes news stories, reports, encyclopedia articles, and essays. The writer's emphasis is on the topic; the approach is objective, and the content is factual.

Persuasive Writing. Persuasion seeks to convince. Editorials, ads, sermons, and fund solicitations are all examples of persuasive writing. The emphasis is on the reader or listener, who is urged to accept an idea or to take an action. Because of this emphasis, the credibility of the writer is highly important. He or she must carefully mix factual evidence and emotional appeals.

One Subject: Four Aims

A good way to illustrate for students the differences among the aims is to suggest a single topic and recast it for varying purposes. Let's say the general subject is boys entering a pageant intended for girls: the Miss Hobart High contest, the Homecoming Queen election, the Strawberry Princess competition, and so on.

- **Expressive: A Personal Narrative.** Darryl, in a paper titled "Sexism on All Sides, " writes in the first person about entering the Miss Hobart High contest: why he decided to do it, how people reacted, what happened, how he felt as a contestant, and what he learned.

- **Creative: A Limerick.** Darryl recaps his pageant experience in an amusing series of limericks.

- **Informative: A Report.** Darryl researches the trend and reports his findings. He notes similar contests throughout the nation, the stated motives of the young men, and reactions to the young mens' participation.

- **Persuasive: A Letter to the Editor.** Darryl writes to both the school and city newspapers, calling for the abolition of the Miss Hobart High contest. He argues that the contest is sexist (there is no "Mr." Hobart High), demeaning (beauty, rather than intelligence or achievement, is emphasized), frivolous (the winner has no duties), and a waste of funds.

The Communication Process

Concrete examples like the ones above reinforce for students the fundamental elements of verbal communication—a **writer**, a **subject**, an **audience**, and **language**—as well as the dynamic relationships among the four elements. As the purpose changes, the main focus shifts from the writer (Darryl) to language (the poetry), to the subject matter (challenges to traditionally female pageants), to the audience (newspaper readers and their opinions).

The Modes

A knowledge of basic aims is not enough, of course, to make students accomplished writers. Even with a subject, a purpose, and an audience, students have to know something about the forms, or modes, of writing: *narration, description, classification,* and *evaluation*.

In the *English Workshop* lessons, students are guided to write effectively in different modes. In an expressive essay, for example, students may need to use narration. They're prompted to describe situations, to recall vivid sensory details, and to order events chronologically. Students learn how the choices and order of details mark different approaches to a subject—how such choices make for an effective comparison (*classification*), review (*evaluation*), or character sketch (*description*).

THE WRITING PROCESS

Writing is more than the isolated moment of physically putting words on paper. It is the dynamic sum of all the moments of analysis, invention, discovery, decision, and even daydreaming that transpire before a writer says, "I'm finished."

Aspects of the Writing Process

The study of writers and their writing activities has shown a common process composed of a series of stages: **prewriting, writing, evaluating and revising, proofreading and publishing**. The writing process is not inflexible, however. Individual writers develop their own styles and variations of the process. For example, one writer may make extensive prewriting notes, while another may take a walk in the woods and then immediately start writing a first draft.

Researchers have also discovered that the writing process is recursive, not linear. In other words, a writer doesn't necessarily proceed in a straight line from prewriting to drafting to evaluating, and so forth. Quite often the writer doubles back, going from drafting back to prewriting to get more ideas, or from evaluation back to drafting to add missing material.

All writers benefit from an understanding of the writing process. Knowing and practicing the basic steps helps writers (especially beginning writers) become more comfortable with writing and learn to experiment with their own abilities.

Prewriting

Prewriting really means pre*drafting*. Prewriting encompasses finding a topic, considering audience and purpose, generating or gathering ideas, and organizing those ideas. It's a stage that beginning writers may fear, avoid, or shortchange. Often, writers are helped immeasurably just by learning that prewriting *is* part of the writing process.

Ideas. A basic prewriting task is identifying ideas for writing. On pages 1–9, *English Workshop*

discusses techniques for finding ideas. Students can use these techniques again and again to generate ideas for subjects or topics and for details related to their topics. Most important, students' topics will reflect their individual interests so that they *own* the writing. To ensure that students are able to refer to these techniques from time to time, they may want to add pages 1–9 to a writing notebook.

Purpose and Audience. Every act of writing has two purposes, a specific one (e.g., to get a refund for a concert ticket) and a general one (e.g., an aim for writing). Chapters 4–7 of *English Workshop* reflect the four basic aims:

- to express oneself
- to create literature
- to inform
- to persuade

> **"**Writing is the dynamic sum of all the moments of analysis, invention, discovery, decision, and even daydreaming that transpire before a writer says, 'I'm finished.'**"**

While a piece of writing can combine aims, one aim almost always predominates; focusing on that primary aim helps students to determine what and how they will write.

Every act of writing has an audience, even if it's only the writer himself or herself. Student writers need to have and believe in an audience other than a teacher. Making an audience real—that is, knowing who they are, what they know and don't know, what they expect, and what they like— guides students in choosing content, vocabulary, sentence style, and tone. A flesh-and-blood audience is one strength of classroom writing groups: Students find out how their peers react to their words. Often, they're surprised!

Organization. With goals decided and information accumulated, the students' next step is organizing. Students assess their information and make a plan, which may be a rough list, a more structured outline, or a graphic device such as a time line or chart. Part of the writing process is learning common organizational techniques (chronological order, order of importance, and so on) that work well with particular types of writing. Each *English Workshop* writing lesson, for example, offers students a visual organizer within which to arrange the paper's details.

Writing

Remind students that drafting is discovery, not the delivery of an error-free paper. Students can follow their written plans but should feel free to make changes and "mistakes." Their object is to get their ideas into sentences and paragraphs. Faulty grammar, usage, and mechanics can be fixed later. *No first draft is a last draft.*

Evaluating and Revising

Now comes a twofold stage: judging, then changing. Writers must evaluate what's wrong (and what's right) in their writing before revising it. In the "Aims for Writing" chapters, the "Questions for Evaluation" portion of each *English Workshop* lesson shows how specific criteria can aid both self-review and peer review. Then students can undertake the basic acts of revision: adding, cutting, replacing, and reordering.

Proofreading and Publishing

Most writers revise more than once. They may even start over, in whole or in part. But with a final, clean copy in hand, the last step is *proofreading.* Students should think of proofreading as a crucial polishing: catching any remaining mistakes in grammar, usage, or mechanics. The "Guidelines for Proofreading" on page 16 in *English Workshop* can be used as a checklist for all papers.

Finally, if the process of writing is to be completed, its result should be *published.* An audience should read (or listen to) what has been written. As the publishing suggestions in the lessons show, students can share their writing in many ways: sending it to a newspaper, reading it aloud to a club, mailing it to someone who helped in the writing, or showing it to another teacher.

STYLES OF LEARNING

People differ in the ways they receive and process information. They tend to channel information through one, or sometimes a combination of two or three, of the learning modalities—auditory, visual, tactile/kinesthetic. For example, students whose main channel for receiving information is auditory would especially benefit from a class discussion of sentence parts. Visual learners might prefer highlighting sentence parts in various colors. Manipulating the parts of sentences on tagboard strips would be an effective method for tactile/kinesthetic learners.

The following chart of patterns of learning shows how students remember information best. If you observe these patterns in your students, you might want to include different learning modalities in your lesson plans.

VISUAL LEARNER	AUDITORY LEARNER	TACTILE/KINESTHETIC LEARNER
Likes written directions	Follows oral directions well	Needs to write directions down
Benefits from movies, slides, or television	Benefits from tapes, records, or radio	Benefits from clapping or other rhythm activities
Enjoys drawing, painting, and working with patterns, maps, and diagrams	Enjoys group discussions, telling stories, and hearing other points of view	Enjoys working with hands or body, chalkboard activities, computers, typing, acting, floor games
Responds to facial expressions and body language	Responds to voice tone and rhythm	Responds to body language
Needs written praise, such as comments on papers, self-stick notes	Needs oral praise	Needs appropriate physical rewards, such as a pat on the back

IDEAS FOR ASSESSMENT: HOLISTIC SCORING AND PORTFOLIOS

Every developing writer needs the feedback a teacher can provide by praising, questioning, and helping to identify problems. But attempting to give students feedback can create other problems. First, it can be extremely time-consuming. Second, it can work against students' understanding of writing as a process. Students may become fixated on the end product. Teachers and researchers are finding ways to keep the paper load manageable and to give students solid feedback without focusing attention solely on grades.

Holistic Scoring

Holistic scoring is a method of evaluation that focuses on the *whole* of a student's paper. The evaluator does not write comments or score the work's separate aspects, such as main ideas, organization, or grammar. A single score indicates the level of competence, sometimes using a number (with 0 or 1 the lowest score and 4 or 5 the highest) or a designation (low, average, or high).

Yet holistic scoring, which is also called general impression, is not vague or subjective, because each scoring level has written, descriptive criteria. (For an example, see the scoring scales in this Answer Key.)

The first step in effective holistic scoring, then, is determining criteria. While a single scale of basic criteria (content, organization, sentence variety, etc.) may be used for all papers, criteria specific to each assignment give students more information. The scales in the *English Workshop* Answer Key are one source of holistic criteria, and the "Questions for Evaluation" in each lesson are other valuable resources.

While the holistic method won't replace more detailed evaluations, it does have benefits beyond its speed.

- It helps students see writing as a synergistic whole, a total effect not reducible to its parts.
- The scoring scale gives students clear information about their work and a vocabulary for discussion.
- Students are usually less intimidated by an overall "impression" than by extensive markings or a letter grade.

Portfolios

Portfolio assessment is another popular method of evaluating student writing. Like a visual artist's portfolio, a student writer's portfolio is a representative collection of work. What is considered representative, however, varies greatly from teacher to teacher and from school to school. Sometimes *portfolio* denotes nothing more than a folder in which students keep all their work— prewriting, drafts, revisions, and finished papers—for the entire year. According to one common definition, however, a portfolio has the following distinguishing elements:

- **Choice.** Students (and sometimes teachers) select the pieces of writing they want to include. The teacher determines the types of items for the portfolios, depending on the course goals, but students decide which particular pieces to include.

- **Process.** Portfolios are not limited to finished papers. These writing collections include evidence of each student's individual writing process; this evidence may include every scrap of paper from prewriting to a complete essay as well as isolated exploratory writing or exercises. Portfolios also represent work over a period of time.

- **Self-Reflection.** Portfolios are annotated. They include students' written reflections about their writings, about their strategies as writers, and about the changes in both over time. (A portfolio may also include the teacher's written responses or student-teacher exchanges.)

Design and Management. The specific contents of writing portfolios can be adapted to the needs of a particular school or teacher. But advance planning of the contents is necessary. A portfolio system should have a table of contents that makes clear each element of the portfolio. For example, it might include

- an introduction (or afterword) in which the student discusses the whole portfolio
- two completed essays (persuasion, expressive writing, etc.), one with all working notes and drafts
- "Writer's Choice" (best or most meaningful writing), with explanation
- "Teacher's Choice," with explanation

Each student might even include his or her *least* satisfactory writing, with a rationale.

While maintaining the portfolio should be each student's responsibility, the portfolio is shared with and is open to the teacher. Portfolios are a form of publishing to be used in writing groups, in displays, and with home audiences.

Assessment. Because portfolios are comprehensive yet selective, structured yet participatory, they offer a natural avenue of assessment. Many possibilities exist for you to personalize the assessment of your students' portfolios:

- Designing a portfolio with the idea that its full contents will be evaluated
- Designating certain parts for evaluation
- Assessing at specified intervals or at year-end
- Combining portfolio assessment with other forms of assessment

Exactly *how* you assess the pieces in a portfolio will vary as well. Perhaps, in cooperation with your students, you can decide which pieces will receive a grade, which a holistic score, which a simple check-off for inclusion, etc.

Even though they offer advantages for assessment, portfolios should not be tied too tightly to a grade. Students should see the portfolios first as their own personal record, resource, and achievement. Students should not just fill the portfolios but should use and learn from them.

COOPERATIVE LEARNING

More and more often, teachers are urged to have students work in pairs or groups. Collaboration not

> **"Students should see the portfolios first as their own personal record, resource, and achievement. Portfolios give students a sense of themselves as working writers."**

4

only yields higher individual achievement but also improves social skills and fosters responsibility for learning.

Yet putting cooperative learning into practice is not a simple matter of grouping students and saying, "Get to work!" Here are some ideas for creating a cooperative classroom.

Who, How Many, and for How Long?

Size. Neither research nor experience has produced absolutes about group size or formation. Generally, though, teachers who use groups recommend a minimum of four students and a maximum of six. Pairs may be useful in early work to get students accustomed to working together and in some specific activities such as proofreading; but pairs might not generate the creative sparks that groups can.

Structure. Some teachers favor a random grouping method, such as counting off, to create heterogeneous mixes. Others appoint students to groups after considering student proficiencies, diversities, and leadership. Letting students form their own groups is less common, but some teachers do so, believing that students naturally form workable ensembles.

Duration. Groups do not need to stay together for an entire term or year. However, don't reorganize them too often. Members need sufficient time to get to know each other and to contribute equally. You might use standing groups for core work and develop new configurations for special activities.

What Activities?

With time and experience, teachers often find ways to transform favorite assignments and classwork from individual to collaborative work. Here are some general suggestions.

1. **Peer Response, Revising, and Proofreading.** These are probably the most familiar cooperative activities. Getting feedback on drafts helps writers, as does proofreading the drafts of others. Actually revising together to rework the draft is another possible step.

2. **Group Prewriting and Writing.** Finding, choosing, and narrowing topics are all good collaborative projects. When you assign a research paper or a persuasive paper, for example, each student will get more ideas by listening to others. Also, give students chances to be coauthors. For example, you might start by asking pairs of students to coauthor a paragraph (you might supply the same data to the whole class). Afterward, be sure to have a discussion about the process: who did what, what the benefits and problems were, and what personal insights each student had.

3. **Learning Teams and Expert Groups.** Students can study for quizzes and tests in teams, helping each other master the material. Expert groups can research a topic and present their findings to the class or to other groups. The students learn by researching, as well as by teaching one another.

4. **Jigsawing.** Jigsawing is actually a pattern for disseminating new learning. Students break up tasks (summarizing textbook chapters, researching rhetorical techniques, etc.), and then teach each other. Simple jigsawing occurs in a single group. Group jigsawing is accomplished by forming second-level groups. Within each original group, students count off and then regroup according to their numbers. Then all "one's" form a new group, all "two's," and so on. Each student teaches the new material to the second group.

How to Manage?

Spelling Things Out. Clear instructions are important in cooperative learning, particularly in early trials. Develop written guidelines requiring students to

- keep work and comments focused on the task, not on people
- combine criticism with concrete suggestions and positive observations
- frequently paraphrase others' points and explanations

Describe the specific product (not necessarily a tangible one) expected of the group work; also list steps, tasks, and time limits. Eventually you will be able to manage the groups' activities more informally. At first, though, a written reference keeps students on track and heads off confusion or disputes.

Establishing Roles. Functional roles in groups are a recorder or reporter who takes notes and speaks for the group (two different students could serve), someone who collects needed classroom materials, and possibly a leader or manager. Let students assign these roles and suggest others.

Facilitating. During group work, the teacher must be on the periphery of the action. As a facilitator, your job is to move freely among groups to pose questions, suggest tactics, and answer legitimate questions.

Above all, have patience. A certain amount of digression as students work is all right. In the beginning, peer responses such as "I don't like this part" will be typical. As you ask questions and model responses, students' responses will become more concrete.

Evaluating. A group grade or some other form of evaluation for a collaborative project not only helps students' commitment and cohesion but also shapes their attitude toward cooperative learning. Depending on the product, you may

- give a group grade
- give a group grade plus individual grades
- create a class (audience) evaluation form for oral reports
- form panels of peer reviewers

Whatever assessment method you choose, clearly state it, along with any evaluation criteria, before work starts.

Students will probably feel anxious about grades that hinge on others' work, and that anxiety should be addressed in class. You can help students to see the positive aspects of collaboration. In their lives after school, they will be working collaboratively in their jobs. Life and work are filled with the need to cooperate with others.

> **❝Students become active learners rather than passive ones. They look for errors or weaknesses, decide how to fix the problems, and try new syntactic effects.❞**

INTEGRATING GRAMMAR, USAGE, AND MECHANICS WITH WRITING

An integrated language arts curriculum, in some form or another, is now familiar in schools and textbooks. Reading, writing, speaking, listening, and viewing are linked because all reinforce one another to develop literacy. In addition, more and more educators are stressing the integration of instruction in grammar, usage, and mechanics with instruction in reading and writing.

Seizing the Moment. This idea is another manifestation of the "teachable moment": Learning within a *context*—a real situation—is more relevant, more personal, and thus more lasting. For example, teaching the forms of the verb *be* is a natural spinoff when students are revising their drafts for strong verb choices.

Using Research. Research supports the integrated approach by showing that the skill-and-drills method of teaching grammar, usage, and mechanics has real limitations. Many students who pass mastery tests still can't apply the skills. But how can teachers teach differently? With increasing frequency, researchers, teachers, and textbook writers offer concrete strategies for integrating the language arts.

Lesson Ideas

Here are some general tips for developing an integrated program in which lessons in grammar, usage, and mechanics are keyed to writing assignments.

1. Match instruction to the specific writing assignment whenever possible. A cause-and-effect essay, for instance, is a good opportunity to teach adverb clauses, which express relationship.

2. Use students' drafts as a source of teaching topics. Almost any grammar instruction can be relevant to the writing lesson if the examples, whether problems or successes, come from the students' own work. Take advantage of portfolios to find fragments, overuse of passive voice, and other problem areas that the whole class can examine, discuss, and revise.

3. Reserve instruction for the revising and proofreading stages. Any nervousness about correctness should not inhibit free drafting. The skill or concept will suggest the timing. For example, an explanation of adverb clauses may clarify meaning during revision; an explanation of subject-verb agreement or capitalization can wait until the proofreading stage.

4. Move from identification to participation to instruction. One good pattern for teaching is to

- identify briefly, with some examples, the topic or element (punctuation of dialogue; dangling modifiers)
- have students find and discuss instances of that topic or element in their papers
- present a fuller lesson on the topic or element, moving directly to students' revising or proofreading

5. Have students keep personal checklists for editing. As students uncover their own problem areas or learn new skills that they want to retain, they can build individual final checklists to use with subsequent papers. A few possibilities for topics keyed to types of writing are

- **Cause and effect:** adverb clauses; subordinating conjunctions and conjunctive adverbs
- **Cause and effect; problem solving:** the *affect-effect* distinction; parallelism

- **Comparison and contrast:** degrees of comparison
- **Narratives:** active voice and passive voice; pronoun case; pronoun reference
- **Process explanations:** colons; items in a series
- **Writing about literature; research reports:** punctuating quotations; incorporating quotations into sentences
- **Writing about literature; reviews:** the *allusion-illusion* distinction; punctuating titles of works; present (historical/literary) tense versus past tense
- **Creative writing:** punctuating dialogue; fragments
- **Journalistic reporting:** appositives; proper nouns and adjectives
- **Description:** parts of speech—adjectives, adverbs, verbs, nouns

Appeal and Advantages

While no new pedagogy will make every student love infinitives, integrating grammar with students' own writing will make the instruction far more interesting than will out-of-context drills. The advantages for students' achievement are numerous.

Rather than learning a string of concepts to be applied later, students deal with problems as they occur and with skills when they are needed. Students recognize—in a year-long continuum of learning—that grammar, usage, and mechanics are useful and necessary to meaning.

Students become active learners rather than passive ones. They look for errors or weaknesses, decide how to fix the problems, and try new syntactic effects. Students become critical thinkers by applying evaluative criteria to their own writing.

MULTICULTURALISM

The United States is becoming increasingly diverse, both ethnically and culturally. In fact, the Census Bureau projects that by the year 2050, non-Hispanic whites will make up only about 53 percent of the U.S. population. Hispanics will comprise 23 percent, African Americans 16 percent, Asian Americans 10 percent, and American Indians slightly more than 1 percent.

As educators, we know the importance of preparing our students to live in our changing society. We want our students to understand and take pride in their own unique ethnic and cultural heritage. We also want them to appreciate the shared cultural heritage of the United States.

To help you meet the needs of students in a multicultural society, *English Workshop* provides culturally diverse topics in assignments, exercises, examples, and models. It is our hope that such topics will provide support for your efforts to build your students' self-esteem and to foster a sense of community in your classroom and our society.

CHAPTER 1:
THE WRITING PROCESS

PREWRITING: FINDING IDEAS
EXERCISE 1, page 1
(Answers will vary. Commend work that shows thoughtfulness and creativity.)

EXERCISE 2, page 2
(Answers will vary. Commend students who write in their journals daily and include ideas or information important to them.)

EXERCISE 3, page 3
(Answers will vary. Commend work that shows an effort to let ideas flow freely. Do not judge the work on mechanics, spelling, or form. Emphasize that prewriting is a creative process and that there will be time later to correct errors.)

PREWRITING: BRAINSTORMING AND CLUSTERING
EXERCISE 4, page 5
(Answers will vary. Commend partners who listen to and consider each other's ideas.)

EXERCISE 5, page 7
(Answers will vary. Point out that clustering can be an effective idea-gathering tool because it lets people's ideas flow freely.)

PREWRITING: ASKING QUESTIONS
EXERCISE 6, page 8
(Answers will vary. A possible response is given.)

Event: The Korean War

Who fought in the war?
What were the major battles of the war?
Where did the fighting take place?
When did the war begin and end?
Why was it fought?
How did the war come to an end?

EXERCISE 7, page 9
(Answers will vary. Commend answers that are full of sensory details. Also commend imaginative "What if" questions.)

PREWRITING: ARRANGING IDEAS
EXERCISE 8, page 10
(Answers will vary. Commend answers in which details are first arranged in a clear spatial order, then are arranged in a clear logical order.)

WRITING A FIRST DRAFT
EXERCISE 9, page 11
(Answers will vary. Satisfactory first drafts will follow the prewriting plan. Commend, however, logical changes and new approaches.)

EVALUATING AND REVISING
EXERCISE 10, page 13
(Answers will vary. Commend evaluations that offer positive and specific observations and suggestions.)

A.

1. not very interesting—too unfocused
2. yes: Columbus may not have been the first European to discover this hemisphere.
3. no: The last detail is misplaced.

B.

How is the fact about Columbus relevant? Other facts are clearly related.

You open with an interesting fact.

Do you mean many of the Indians live in the Petén, or that the people living in the Petén are Indians?

Which do you think is the most important point? You might use it in the first sentence. Choose one of the types of ordering and stick with it.

EXERCISE 11, page 15
(Answers will vary. Commend work that shows use of the four techniques for revision.)

PROOFREADING AND PUBLISHING
EXERCISE 12, page 17
(Answers will vary.)

Marny and I built a treehouse for a local Head Start center. It is the project that I worked on for most of this year. Neither Marny nor I had ever built anything before or done any carpentry. We got some advice from my father, who is a carpenter, but we did all the work ourselves. The materials we had were sturdy, treated pine boards; redwood stain; nails; bolts; and dowels. The treehouse took three weeks to build on weekends and in the evenings, and it should last for at least ten years.

EXERCISE 13, page 18
(Answers will vary. Commend answers that suggest a variety of publishing venues.)

1. an oral report for your class or another class, English/Spanish magazines
2. a family newsletter, a letter to a friend
3. a local newspaper, a letter to a city council member or the mayor

CHAPTER 2:
PARAGRAPH WORKSHOPS

USES OF PARAGRAPHS
EXERCISE 1, page 20
(Answers will vary. The exercise will be successfully completed if examples include each of the four uses of paragraphs and list each source. Praise responses that name additional uses of paragraphs.)

UNITY

EXERCISE 2, page 22
1. California is about the size of Sweden.
2. Stamp collecting and coin collecting are popular hobbies.
3. Planting a tree can also be a rewarding experience.
4. Another bird that moves fast is the ostrich.
5. The waters off this western shore are usually warm.

COHERENCE: ORDER OF IDEAS

EXERCISE 3, page 24
(Answers may vary. Possible responses are given.)
1. 1, 4, 6, 5, 7, 8, 9, 3, 10, 2; chronological order
2. 2, 1, 4, 3, 5; logical order

COHERENCE: CONNECTIONS BETWEEN IDEAS

EXERCISE 4, page 26

	DIRECT REFERENCES	*TRANSITIONAL WORDS*
1.	Thomas Jefferson	first; in
2.	he; there; it; President's House	when; however
3.	Jefferson; he	Although; when
4.	his; desk	
5.	It; his	also
6.	his	on; and; in; and
7.	Jefferson; his; he his; it	When; in; out of; and; around
8.	He; disorganized; he	just; when
9.	no planning ahead	There
10.	Jefferson; he	Nevertheless

USING DESCRIPTION

EXERCISE 5, page 27
(Answers will vary. Commend answers that list sensory details in sensible spatial order. There should be enough details to give a clear picture of the subject.)

USING EVALUATION

EXERCISE 6, page 28
(Answers will vary. Students should follow the example's structure, state an opinion, and offer at least two logical reasons supporting that opinion for each of the three topics.)

USING NARRATION

EXERCISE 7, page 30
(Answers will vary. Commend answers that list actions, steps, or causes and effects in a sensible order. For the suggested assignments, chronological order will make the most sense. The details should provide enough information to clearly tell a story, explain a process, or explain causes and effects.)

USING CLASSIFICATION

EXERCISE 8, page 32
(Answers will vary. Commend students for cooperative work. Paragraph 1 should be developed by listing examples of sports within each of the three categories. Paragraph 2 should be developed by describing a favorite sport and contrasting it with other sports. Paragraph 3 should be developed by identifying two or three similarities and two or three differences in sports of today and sports seventy-five years from now.)

CHAPTER 3: COMPOSITION WORKSHOPS

THE THESIS STATEMENT

EXERCISE 1, page 34
(Answers will vary. Commend work that shows thoughtfulness and creativity.)
1. Watching violence on television can affect children's behavior.
2. Working as a lifeguard has taught me self-reliance and self-confidence.

EXERCISE 2, page 34
(Answers will vary. A possible response is given.)
Some commonly heard advice for taking care of a cold is actually good advice.

PLANNING A COMPOSITION

EXERCISE 3, page 36
(Answers will vary. A possible response is given.)

Donating services

Teens can teach reading to homeless adults at a shelter.

Teens can tutor homeless children in shelters with established programs.

Lawyers can provide free legal assistance to people in shelters for the homeless.

Tradespeople can offer their services to projects such as Habitat for Humanity.

Donating goods and funds

After collecting used books and toys from their homes, from friends, and from neighbors, groups can donate them to shelters.

School and church groups can organize food or clothing drives.

School and scouting groups can raise money for local shelters by holding bake sales and service auctions.

EXERCISE 4, page 36
(Answers will vary. A possible response is given.)

Title: Donating Goods and Services to Help the Homeless

Thesis Statement: Concerned individuals can volunteer their services or collect goods and funds to help the homeless.

I. Volunteering services
   A. Teens
      1. Tutor children
      2. Teach reading
   B. Adults
      1. Lawyers
      2. Tradespeople
II. Collecting goods and funds
   A. Toy and book collections
   B. Food/clothing drives
   C. Fundraising activities
      1. Bake sales
      2. Service auctions

EXERCISE 5, page 39
(Answers will vary. Possible responses are given.)

1. Open with a question *or* an anecdote.
2. Open with an unusual fact *or* with a description.
3. Open by directly addressing reader.
4. Open with a stand on an issue.

EXERCISE 6, page 40
(Answers will vary. This exercise will be satisfactorily completed if the student uses one of the eight techniques listed in the lesson to write an introduction. The introduction should be interesting and should provide a thesis statement.)

WRITING CONCLUSIONS
EXERCISE 7, page 42
(Answers will vary. Possible responses are given.)

1. Refer to introduction and restate thesis.
2. Call readers to action.
3. Summarize main points and make a prediction.
4. Restate thesis.

EXERCISE 8, page 43
(Answers will vary. This exercise will be satisfactorily completed if the student uses one of the six techniques listed in the lesson to write a conclusion. The conclusion should also sum up the main idea and clearly indicate that the composition is complete.)

CHAPTER 4:
EXPRESSING YOURSELF

A HIGH SCHOOL REFLECTION
THINKING ABOUT THE MODEL, page 46
(Answers will vary. Possible responses are given.)

1. Yes. The first sentence establishes the writer's enthusiasm, and the following descriptions set lively scenes. The mention of "whining," and other comments, also shows a sense of humor.
2. They show how important the marching band was to the writer, both as a fantasy and as a serious pursuit.
3. Some possible examples: on my uncle's shoulders; Kids started clapping along; blue and gold uniforms; We rattled the windows! stumbled along, my music was bobbing up and down; frozen fingers didn't help; I . . . slammed into a senior; my face felt like fire.
4. Some possible examples: "To be able to play that great music *and* wear a uniform *and* make complicated patterns *and* get cheers—well, you get the picture." ". . . left, right, stop, turn, whatever—in rhythm. Ha!" (Students may also cite colloquial expressions such as "I was hooked" and "Drilling . . . was something else.")

5. During drill he felt awkward, frustrated, nervous, and embarrassed. After he quit he felt regretful but pretended not to care or to feel superior.
6. He should have tried longer and been unashamed to ask for help, rather than let an opportunity pass by.

ASSIGNMENT: WRITING A HIGH SCHOOL REFLECTION, page 48
TO THE TEACHER: The following is a grading scale you may wish to use in evaluating a student's narrative.

SCORE POINT 4

4= The essay's beginning is interesting and includes necessary background information.

The essay presents a significant high school experience and arranges events in a clear order.

Descriptions of events, people, and places include effective sensory details.

Thoughts and feelings are woven effectively throughout the essay.

The essay's closing is satisfying and makes the meaning of the experience clear.

SCORE POINT 3

3= The essay's beginning is fairly interesting and includes necessary background information.

The essay presents a significant high school experience and arranges events in a clear order.

Descriptions of events, people, and places include fairly effective sensory details.

Thoughts and feelings are woven fairly effectively throughout the essay.

The essay's closing is fairly satisfying and makes the meaning of the experience clear.

SCORE POINT 2

2= The essay's beginning is not very interesting or does not include necessary background information.

The main experience of the essay is unclear, or its events are difficult to follow.

Descriptions of events, people, and places include few effective sensory details.

Thoughts and feelings are not woven throughout the essay.

The essay's closing is not satisfying or does not make the meaning of the experience clear.

SCORE POINT 1

1= The essay's beginning is not interesting and does not include necessary background information.

The essay does not present a significant high school experience or arrange events in a clear order.

Descriptions of events, people, and places include almost no effective sensory details.

Thoughts and feelings are seldom included in the essay.

The essay's closing is not satisfying and does not make the meaning of the experience clear.

CHAPTER 5:
CREATIVE WRITING

A TELEVISION SCRIPT
THINKING ABOUT THE MODEL, page 58
(Answers will vary. Possible responses are given.)

1. The speaker's name is printed in capital letters followed by a colon. A new paragraph begins whenever speakers change.
2. *The dog's actions:* "This dog destroyed my suit . . ."; "It is a vicious, uncontrollable beast . . ."; "Why would a dog chew up a three-hundred-dollar suit?"; "He knocked over a paint can and stepped in the paint. Then he tracked the paint . . ."; "And the eighteen roses he dug up in the garden"; ". . . the dog drove her cat Sprinkles crazy."
   Sandra's casual language: "Gee, Mr. Markowitz"; "Yeah, gray"; "I mean, you can't expect him to understand about prices and things"; "Sounds kinda nice."
   Sandra's sarcasm: "Certainly looks like a killer"; "Well, he's a dog"; "I'll hold the beast while you leave."
3. in capital letters
4. *A setting (location):* FRONT OFFICE OF AN ANIMAL SHELTER.
   A character's costume: <u>MARKOWITZ</u> IS WEARING A SUIT WITH A TORN JACKET AND PANTS LEG.
   A character's emotion or reaction: **MARKOWITZ** (OBVIOUSLY UPSET).
   An object a character uses: (TAKING PEN AND PAPER).
   How or where a character should move: (POINTING TO HIS FACE).
   A change in camera position: PULL BACK TO INT. FRONT OFFICE OF ANIMAL SHELTER.
5. *CUT:* CUT TO MARKOWITZ, WHO BOLTS OUT OF CHAIR AND GETS BEHIND IT.
   INT.: INT. FRONT OFFICE OF AN ANIMAL SHELTER.
   SFX: SFX DOGS AND CATS.
   C-U: C-U OF POSTER READING . . .
6. Father was promised a gentle, easy-going dog but is getting a "vicious, uncontrollable beast."

ASSIGNMENT: WRITING A TELEVISION SCRIPT, page 60

TO THE TEACHER: The following is a grading scale you may wish to use in evaluating a student's script.

SCORE POINT 4
4 = The characters are believable and vivid and speak naturally.
The script introduces a strong central conflict.
Set directions effectively describe sound effects, music, setting, characters, and camera work.
The closing creates strong tension or curiosity.
The script follows proper format.

SCORE POINT 3
3 = The characters are fairly believable and vivid and speak fairly naturally.
The script introduces a fairly strong central conflict.
Set directions fairly effectively describe sound effects, music, setting, characters, and camera work.
The closing creates tension or curiosity.
The script follows proper format.

SCORE POINT 2
2 = The characters are sometimes not believable and vivid and sometimes do not speak naturally.
The script's central conflict is weak.
Set directions omit some needed descriptions of sound effects, music, setting, characters, and camera work.
The closing creates only weak tension or curiosity.
The script shows errors in format.

SCORE POINT 1
1 = The characters are not believable and vivid and do not speak naturally.
The script does not introduce a central conflict.
Set directions do not effectively describe sound effects, music, setting, characters, and camera work.
The closing does not create tension or curiosity.
The script does not follow proper format.

CHAPTER 6:
INFORMING OTHERS

A RÉSUMÉ
THINKING ABOUT THE MODEL, page 68
(Answers will vary. Possible responses are given.)

1. JOB DESIRED, EDUCATION, WORK EXPERIENCE, OTHER EXPERIENCE AND SKILLS, REFERENCES
2. She mentions three possible job areas (advertising, publishing, or journalism) and specifies her skill areas (graphic arts and editing).
3. She lists her job duties.
4. She includes her volunteer work coordinating a food pantry. She lists business skills, machine operation.
5. Miriam Taylor is her current employer. James Mendoza is her graphic arts teacher.

ASSIGNMENT: WRITING A RÉSUMÉ, page 69

TO THE TEACHER: An evaluation scale is not appropriate for this résumé assignment. You can give credit for the completion of the assignment, or you can use the Questions for Evaluation on page 73 to assign a student a grade of Satisfactory or Unsatisfactory.

CHAPTER 7:
PERSUADING OTHERS

A LETTER OF APPLICATION
THINKING ABOUT THE MODEL, page 78
(Answers will vary. Possible responses are given.)

1. apprentice carpenter; in the first paragraph
2. The writer has taken beginning and advanced woodworking classes. He has done "odd jobs" in carpentry. He can read blueprints. He also owns carpentry tools.
3. He is good at math and does bookkeeping for his parents' restaurant.
4. the hard work and discipline of two years on the track team
5. He offers references, supplies a telephone number, and explains when he's available for part- and full-time work.

ASSIGNMENT: WRITING A LETTER OF APPLICATION, page 79
TO THE TEACHER: The following is a grading scale you may wish to use in evaluating a student's letter.

SCORE POINT 4

4= The letter's opening clearly identifies the job.

The letter provides full details about the writer's qualifications for the job.

The letter strongly expresses the writer's interest in the work.

The letter's ending offers to provide references. It supplies information about contacting the writer or about the writer's availability.

The letter follows proper business form.

SCORE POINT 3

3= The letter's opening identifies the job fairly clearly.

The letter lacks a few details about the writer's qualifications for the job.

The letter fairly strongly expresses the writer's interest in the work.

The letter's ending offers to provide references. It supplies some information about contacting the writer or about the writer's availability.

The letter almost always follows proper business form.

SCORE POINT 2

2= The letter's opening identifies the job but not very clearly.

The letter does not provide enough details about the writer's qualifications for the job.

The letter expresses the writer's interest in the work, but too weakly.

The letter's ending does not offer to provide references, or it does not supply information about contacting the writer or about the writer's availability.

The letter has several errors in business form.

SCORE POINT 1

1= The letter's opening does not identify the job.

The letter does not provide details about the writer's qualifications for the job.

The letter does not express the writer's interest in the work.

The letter's ending does not offer to provide references. It does not supply information about contacting the writer or about the writer's availability.

The letter does not follow business form.

CHAPTER 8:
SENTENCE WORKSHOPS

COORDINATING IDEAS
EXERCISE 1, page 88

1. , but
2. , so
3. , and
4. , yet
5. , but
6. , and
7. , but
8. , so
9. , for
10. , yet

EXERCISE 2, page 88
(Answers will vary. Possible responses are given.)

1. My friend Otis wanted to be a professional dancer, but he teaches school today.
2. I would like to see the play *Our Town*, but I went to see *Cats*.
3. Yukio or Julia could give the report.
4. Sheena said hello to Roger, and he turned around and said, "How are you?"
5. I wasn't tired yesterday, for I took a nap in the afternoon.

SUBORDINATING IDEAS
EXERCISE 3, page 90

1. Whenever I go to San Francisco, I ride the trolley cars.
2. The principal told me that graduation will be held in the gymnasium.
3. After the meeting ended, we served refreshments.
4. I often write to my aunt who lives in Morocco.
5. Sandra said that blue jays and cardinals are Joel's favorite birds.
6. Danny Glover is an actor whom I've seen in two movies.
7. My grandmother told me that this bread contains walnuts and raisins.
8. Sal needs to go to the barber because his hair is in his eyes.
9. I am positive that Monique will be a great president one day.
10. I have a neighbor named Ms. Rego who feeds my cat when I am away.
11. After the storm ended at midnight, branches were scattered in the street.
12. My brother told me that cranberry juice is in the pantry.
13. I admire that woman who is running for mayor.
14. Because Lynn broke her ankle, she needs a plaster cast.
15. Mr. Wong is a teacher whom I think is great.
16. Gerald will be hired for the job if he will go to the interview.
17. I should tell you why I cannot attend this rehearsal.
18. Pam, who is a reporter, enjoys working for the newspaper.

19. We should leave early so that we can arrive on time.
20. Although Harry shopped at the mall, he didn't find the birthday card he wanted.

USING PARALLEL STRUCTURE
EXERCISE 4, page 91
(Answers will vary. Possible responses are given.)

1. During our school vacations, I like bicycling, walking, and swimming at the state park.
2. Marty believes reading a good book is more rewarding than watching television.
3. Hector hopes either to write his entire mystery novel or at least to start it this summer.
4. Ms. Shapiro is recognized for being active in town government and for being a baseball coach.
5. Bonita enjoys studying algebra and earth science.
6. My sister Shanelle would like both to plan the local road races and to run in them.
7. When completing assignments, being accurate and neat is more important than being fast.
8. Old newspapers around the house are not only a mess but also a fire hazard.
9. My sister Sienna likes sailing and canoeing.
10. Neither cleaning the living room nor sweeping the kitchen appeals to Leroy, who is exhausted.

SENTENCE FRAGMENTS AND RUN-ON SENTENCES
EXERCISE 5, page 94
(Answers will vary. Possible responses are given.)

1. She is thankful for her friend Pablo, who told her about the symphony.
2. Pablo, who plays the cello, has been in the symphony for two years.
3. Every Wednesday night when the symphony meets, they use the high school music room.
4. The musicians take turns driving to the evening rehearsals.
5. Last year the symphony traveled to a competition in Canada. They played well and had a wonderful time.
6. The symphony took second place with their performance of Aaron Copland's *Appalachian Spring*.
7. Pablo also played a violin solo. He received a loud round of applause.
8. When they returned home, the symphony gave a concert on the steps of the town hall.
9. The concert drew a large crowd. The audience was quite impressed by the variety of the music and the skill of the musicians.
10. The concert was a success. It raised a lot of money for a local soup kitchen.

UNNECESSARY SHIFTS
EXERCISE 6, page 95
(Answers will vary. Possible responses are given.)

1. Uncle Mateo's chili and cornbread are really delicious.
2. When I went to concerts in the city last summer, I heard great jazz musicians.
3. Ana almost completed the entire obstacle course, but didn't have enough time.

4. Parents should sign permission slips if they want their children to go on the field trip.
5. We traveled to the White Mountains and admired the forests of birch trees.
6. Corky likes the sweaters, socks, and hats at Darla's Boutique.
7. Willis wanted to organize a musical group, but he couldn't find many musicians.
8. As I studied for my biology test, I listened to the howling wind and to the pouring rain.
9. All travelers should check their new schedules if they don't want to miss their trains.
10. My father grows roses and daffodils in his garden.

REVIEW EXERCISE
A., page 97
(Answers will vary. A possible response is given.)

[1] Because it was Independence Day, my town was having a large carnival. [2] A crowd of people gathered, watching hot-air balloons and eating hot dogs. [3] The crowd cheered the balloonists as the balloons filled with heated air and rose into the summer sky.

[4] A person must be a bit of a daredevil if he or she wants to ride in a hot-air balloon. [5] Because they seem dangerous to me, I don't like to ride in hot-air balloons myself. [6] In my opinion, a person has to be crazy to want to go up in one of those things. [7] However, many people enjoy the experience of sailing slowly through the sky and waving to people on the ground below.

[8] Fortunately, no accidents occurred at the Independence Day Race, and all the balloonists and spectators had a good time. [9] The balloons drifted over the park and landed safely across the river on the enormous courthouse lawn. [10] Mr. Haltom, in his large red-white-and-blue balloon, both won the balloon race and received the award as the most skillful balloonist.

B., page 98
(Answers will vary. A possible response is given.)

All fiction writing involves leaps of the imagination. However, the biggest leaps are usually taken by science fiction writers. Writers of science fiction imagine worlds that do not yet exist. They take us on incredible journeys in time and space, deep into the earth, to distant planets, back into the distant past, or forward into the far-off future.

People use the term *science fiction* in different ways. Some people use it to refer to any highly unrealistic or improbable story. However, it is probably best to use the term *fantasy* for those improbable stories that do not contain scientific elements. Most experts would agree that a story needs to involve science if it is to be considered science fiction.

The first outstanding American science fiction writer was Edgar Allan Poe. One of his stories, "The Unparalleled Adventures of One Hans Pfaal," tells about a flight to the moon aboard a hot-air balloon. Poe inspired many imitators, including Jules Verne, who predicted the invention of submarines in his novel *Twenty Thousand Leagues under the Sea*. Other excellent early science fiction writers include H. G. Wells, Edgar Rice Burroughs, and Madeleine L'Engle. Some popular, modern-day science fiction writers include Ray Bradbury, Isaac Asimov, and Virginia Hamilton.

COMBINING BY INSERTING WORDS
EXERCISE 7, page 99
(Answers will vary. Possible responses are given.)
1. Happily, I watched my grandparents dance to their favorite song.
2. Jocelyn is a trustworthy mechanic.
3. My friend Oscar quickly cleaned all the windows.
4. Proudly, June watched her brother dance and sing on the stage.
5. Pia walked slowly to the podium to get her high school diploma.
6. Al planted beautiful shrubbery in his front yard.
7. My father and I had an interesting discussion.
8. My friend Martin skillfully revised his research paper.
9. My new kitten Freckles playfully batted at the rubber ball.
10. Porter nervously began his first day at his new job.
11. Stella gave a large bag of clothing to charity.
12. Maya Angelou spoke inspiringly at the conference.
13. My friend sadly walked around the cafeteria looking for her lost bracelet.
14. We anxiously waited for the train from Memphis to arrive.
15. Max began mowing the lawn yesterday.

COMBINING BY INSERTING PHRASES
EXERCISE 8, page 102
(Answers will vary. Possible responses are given.)
1. We were working hard on our history project.
2. Earl, a former student at Wilson High School, is now an English teacher there.
3. I like the whole-wheat bread made at the local bakery.
4. I went to Marcia's house to help her babysit her brothers the other night.
5. Jamie went to the library on Saturday afternoon.
6. In chemistry class, Jillian learned about measuring the mass of gas.
7. I like those warm woolen sweaters made in a small town in Ireland.
8. Uncle Ernie, being exceptionally healthy, did not catch the flu this year.
9. My friend made low-fat yogurt shakes for an after-school snack.
10. Anita, my youngest sister, painted the outside of the garage.

COMBINING BY COORDINATION AND SUBORDINATION
EXERCISE 9, page 103
(Answers will vary. Possible responses are given.)
1. We can make either a model volcano or a model rain forest for science class.
2. The apartment was noisy, so Esther couldn't fall asleep.
3. Neither the living room nor the kitchen is warm.
4. I wanted to prepare dinner, but nobody else was hungry.
5. Everyone wanted a holiday party, yet only four people offered to help plan the event.
6. Sampson likes to eat fresh spinach and fresh squash.
7. You can take the bus or the train to South Station.
8. The car and the old truck won't start.
9. I am looking forward to spring, for the flowers will be in full bloom.
10. I believe both Avery and Enrico have enormous potential.

EXERCISE 10, page 104
(Answers will vary. Possible responses are given.)
1. Ashley and Carter explained to me why they like to watch science fiction movies.
2. Because it makes his body feel strong and healthy, Franz rides his bike for three miles each day.
3. My sister, who is graduating this year, has decided to become a middle school science teacher.
4. We fed carrots to the baby rabbits, who love this crunchy vegetable.
5. That building, which is going to be a post office, will be completed in about two years.
6. The paper explained why the parade would be postponed.
7. Since she finished medical school, that doctor has been teaching a class about good eating habits.
8. My brother, who wants to go to summer camp, is saving his allowance.
9. A neigbor told me that City Hall is the oldest building in town.
10. The Dahlis, who own one restaurant, are now building another restaurant on Park Drive.

VARYING SENTENCE BEGINNINGS
EXERCISE 11, page 105
(Answers will vary. Possible responses are given.)
1. Suddenly, the baby began to cry.
2. Because it was a big job, Martina helped me with the project.
3. During the night I saw several flashes of lightning.
4. To help that stray puppy, I'll need food and medicine.
5. Before he took up sculpting, my dad was a painter.
6. Running into the gymnasium, Gerardo asked, "Could I be on one of the teams?"
7. Fortunately, Theo brought a bright flashlight.
8. Whenever the weather becomes cold, I scatter birdseed on the ground.
9. Wanting an old book, Diane looked in the telephone directory for used bookstores.
10. To earn enough money for that telescope, I'll need to increase my work hours.
11. When I won the chess tournament, Kyle gave me a pat on the back.
12. When that movie theater closed last summer, I was disappointed.

13. Over the weekend, five of us plan to clip those hedges.
14. Thrilled, I ran to give everyone the good news.
15. Whenever I'm in a difficult situation, I can count on my best friend.

VARYING SENTENCE STRUCTURE

EXERCISE 12, page 108

(Answers will vary. A possible response is given.)

Kabuki is an interesting type of theater that combines song, dance, mime, and elaborate costumes. *Kabuki* is a Japanese word that means "song," "dance," and "skill." Kabuki was started in the sixteenth century by a former Japanese priestess named Okuni. She staged religious dances and performed for audiences in her hometown. Okuni's dancing became popular, so she decided to make her show bigger. She assembled a group of women who had experience with song and dance and taught them her performance. Kabuki theater today is similar to the earliest Kabuki theater in that it still uses singing, dialogue, and a unique type of audience participation. Actors talk to spectators, and the spectators respond with words or by clapping to a rhythm. When Kabuki started, most themes were based on religious teachings, but contemporary events appeared in later Kabuki performances.

EXERCISE 13, page 108

(Answers will vary. Commend responses that use sentences with single-word modifiers, prepositional phrases, participial phrases, appositive phrases, coordinating conjunctions, subordinate clauses, and a variety of sentence beginnings.)

REDUCING WORDINESS

EXERCISE 14, page 109

(Answers will vary. Possible responses are given.)

1. Cousin Estrella and I put the damp sneakers near the heating vent.
2. Chuck, the last person to leave, locked the door and pulled the shades.
3. Before building the doghouse, we sketched pictures of it.
4. I couldn't finish my math homework because I was tired.
5. My knee was scraped after the fall, but I got back on the bicycle.
6. Those are my hiking boots.
7. Kim, born in Korea, would love to travel to her homeland someday soon.
8. Please bring your teacher a note from your parent explaining why you are late.
9. Luckily, when Oliver misplaced his wallet yesterday, he found it right away.
10. That terrific radio show is on every morning and evening.

CHAPTER REVIEW

A., page 111

(Answers will vary. Possible responses are given.)

1. I forgot to water the plant, so it dried out.
2. Writing a poem is as creative an activity as painting a picture.
3. Pauline is not only a great horseback rider but also a great runner.
4. My brother sent his résumé to a company downtown.
5. The dog needs to be groomed and vaccinated.
6. Arthur is helpful not only as a lifeguard but also as a teacher.
7. I want more recipes and more time for preparing meals.
8. Lorna likes basketball better than volleyball.
9. Sam works a paper route on Main Street and Jewett Street.
10. The light bulb burned out, so I changed it.

B., page 111

(Answers will vary. Possible responses are given.)

1. Other people had flown the Atlantic, but he was the first to fly alone.
2. Lindbergh needed a special kind of plane that could carry him nonstop from New York City to Paris.
3. C
4. The trip, which was 3,500 miles long, took thirty-three hours.
5. He landed in Paris, France, to find an excited crowd waiting for him.

C., page 112

(Answers will vary. Possible responses are given.)

1. My friend Magda works at the variety store near the center of town.
2. All I want for lunch is more of that delicious soup.
3. Because we collected cans and bottles all morning, we were able to take a large load to the recycling center.
4. It was a breezy day, so we brought our new blue box kite to the beach.
5. Running after the bus, Lee waved his arms and shouted, "Stop—my book bag!"

D., page 112

(Answers will vary. Possible responses are given.)

1. We refinished the chairs, and Uncle Emil liked them so much that we gave them to him for his birthday.
2. Washing the windows, I stood on a small ladder.
3. Before the hayride, Carmen dressed warmly so she wouldn't get cold.
4. Since the guests arrived early for Thanksgiving dinner, we gave them cheese and crackers.
5. The flowers were wilting, so I changed the water in the vase.
6. Listening to my sister's band, I danced.
7. Because the tomatoes and cucumbers were ripe, we made a big salad.
8. After we were told that the goat at the farm was friendly, we fed him grain.
9. So people would understand the issue, the organization held a press conference.
10. Gabrielle lost her keys in the yard, but she found them.

CHAPTER 9: LANGUAGE WORKSHOPS

THE ORIGINS OF ENGLISH

EXERCISE 1, page 114

(Answers will vary depending on dictionary used. Possible entries are given.)

1. cursus (L), fr. cursus, pp. of currere—to run; course (OF); course (ME)
2. angre (L)—to strangle; angr (ON)—grief, akin to enge (OE)—narrow; anger (ME)—affliction, anger
3. deyja (ON)—to die; dien (ME)
4. porcus (L); porc (OF)—pig; pork (ME)
5. gentilis (L)—of a clan, of the same clan; gentle (OF); gentil (ME)
6. castellum (L)—fortess, castle; castle (ONF); castle (OE); castel (ME)
7. judo (Jpn) judo—ju, soft + do, way
8. judicare (L); jugier (OF); juggen (ME)
9. tomato (Sp) tomate—(Nahuatl) tomal
10. discus (L)—quoit, disk, dish; disc (OE)—plate; dish (ME)
11. hrēod (OE); rede (ME)
12. dǣge (OE)—kneader of bread, akin to dāg (OE)—dough; deyerie (ME), fr. deye (OE)—dairymaid
13. taka (ON); tacan (OE); taken (ME)
14. sæti (ON), akin to sittan (OE)—to sit; sete (ME)
15. fēlagi (ON) fr. fēlag—partnership, fr. fē—cattle, money (akin to OE feoh) + lag—act of laying, akin to licgan (OE)—to lie; fēolaga (OE); felawe (ME)
16. bayou (AmFr)—(Choctaw) bayuk, small stream
17. bullire (L)—to bubble, fr. bulla—bubble; boillir (OF); boilen (ME)
18. hanter (OF), of Gmc origin, akin to hām (OE)—home; haunten (ME)
19. cor (L); courage (OF), fr. cuer—heart; corage (ME)
20. pulver-, pulvis (L)—dust; poudre (OF); poudre (ME)

FORMAL AND INFORMAL ENGLISH

EXERCISE 2, page 116

1. informal	8. formal	15. informal
2. informal	9. informal	16. informal
3. formal	10. formal	17. formal
4. informal	11. formal	18. formal
5. formal	12. informal	19. informal
6. informal	13. informal	20. informal
7. informal	14. formal	

SPECIFIC AND VIVID WORDS

EXERCISE 3, page 117

(Answers will vary. Possible answers are given.)

1. An unexpected thunderstorm spoiled the picnic.
2. Toni's dress is embroidered with an intricate design.
3. The saltwater aquarium contains anemones.
4. "I'll be in charge of the decorations," Sam volunteered.
5. As the hurricane's winds blew harder, the windows rattled in their frames.
6. Tanya and April were exhausted after hiking all day.
7. "Water is rushing into the boat," warned the captain.
8. The carpenter removed the hammer from her workbelt.
9. Suni angrily slammed the door behind her.
10. Suddenly, a Chihuahua came around the corner.
11. The tennis player was ecstatic over her victory.
12. I just read an extremely detailed article about British colonialism.
13. The New Hampshire woods are lush.
14. You look despondent.
15. After she bit into the jalapeño, Celia's eyes watered.
16. We enjoyed seeing old friends at the reunion.
17. The chauffeur will be waiting beside the limousine.
18. Each evening, our dog Melon devours her food.
19. At the end of a long day at school, their teacher sank into her chair.
20. Roses, geraniums, and tulips decorate our backyard.

LEVELS OF MEANING

EXERCISE 4, page 120

(Answers will vary. Possible answers are given.)

1. jabbered—spoke excitedly, talked enthusiastically
2. old-fashioned—classical, nostalgic, sentimental
3. odor—fragrance, perfume
4. congressman—congress person, representative
5. weird—avant garde, eccentric, unusual
6. gossiped about—discussed
7. crazy—mistaken, wrong
8. salesgirl—salesperson, sales assistant
9. Fanatics—Fervent supporters, Firm supporters
10. stewardess—flight attendant
11. at a snail's pace—quite slowly
12. strange—unusual, unique
13. propaganda—publicity
14. firemen—firefighters
15. sloppy—casual
16. Mankind— Human beings, People
17. cautiously—carefully
18. tragic—unfortunate
19. fake—imitation
20. pushy—aggressive

UNCLEAR LANGUAGE

EXERCISE 5, page 122

1. eager	6. predict
2. intensive	7. surprised
3. further	8. incredible
4. illusions	9. effects
5. include	10. modern

EXERCISE 6, page 122

(Answers will vary. Possible answers are given.)

1. Kesha has been extremely industrious.
2. Don't leave me in suspense.
3. The documentary was engrossing.

4. You're talking to the wrong person.
5. The police commissioner vowed that the investigators would be quite thorough in their work.
6. Raymond supported his thesis with historical evidence.
7. At daylight saving time, you need to adjust the hands of the clock.
8. Reggie completed the puzzle and said, "That was easy."
9. "Golf is a complex game," the instructor stated.
10. Marla is an accomplished singer.

CHAPTER REVIEW

A., page 123

(Answers will vary depending on the dictionary used. Possible etymologies are given.)

1. Proto-Indo-European
2. Christianity introduced many Latin words; the Norse invasions from the ninth through eleventh centuries introduced Scandinavian words.
3. It marks the beginning of the Middle English period, during which English was greatly influenced by the French-speaking ruling class.
4. French and Latin
5. Modern English
6. Latin *or* Indo-European
7. French
8. hweogol, hwēol (OE), akin to hvēl (ON)—wheel; wheel (ME)
9. preost (OE); preist (ME)
10. etymologia (L); ethimologie (ME)

B., page 123

(Answers will vary. Possible answers are given.)

1. girls—women
2. impress—express
3. handy—useful
4. honorable—honored
5. intentional—intended
6. widely famed—famous
7. easy—simple
8. confusing—complex, intricate
9. dot—mark, adorn, decorate
10. enlighten—teach

C., page 124

(Answers will vary. Possible answers are given.)

1. She enjoyed success as a writer of books for children and adults.
2. She published her first collection of stories in 1949.
3. (correct)
4. Some of her stories were adaptations of Japanese folktales.
5. The years she spent in an internment camp during World War II also profoundly affected her writing.
6. Following the bombing of Pearl Harbor, the U.S. government imprisoned thousands of Japanese Americans.
7. After five months in one internment camp, the twenty-year-old Uchida and her family were relocated to Topaz, a guarded camp in Utah.
8. (correct)
9. Her parents were released from the camp later that year.
10. After her mother's death in 1966, Uchida wrote *Journey to Topaz: A Story of the Japanese-American Evacuation*, as a tribute to the hardships her parents had experienced.
11. This book was her first about the Japanese-American culture and experience.
12. Since then, she has written many insightful stories about Japanese-American culture.
13. In 1982, Uchida detailed her experiences during the internment in *Desert Exile: The Uprooting of a Japanese-American Family*.
14. Uchida hoped that her writing might give young Japanese Americans a sense of self-esteem.
15. Many important awards show Uchida's success in producing books that respond to young people's need for identity.

CHAPTER 10:
PARTS OF SPEECH

NOUNS

EXERCISE 1, page 126

1. comm.	14. comm.; comp.
2. comm.; comp.	15. prop.; comp.
3. comm.; coll.	16. comm.; coll.
4. comm.	17. comm.; comp.
5. prop.; comp.	18. prop.
6. comm.; comp.	19. comm.; comp.
7. comm.	20. prop.
8. prop.; comp.	21. comm.; comp.
9. comm.; coll.	22. comm.
10. comm.	23. comm.; coll.
11. comm.; comp.	24. comm.
12. prop.; comp.	25. comm.; comp.
13. comm.	

EXERCISE 2, page 126

1. con.; con.	6. abs.; abs.	11. abs.; con.
2. con.; con.	7. con.; con.	12. con.; con.
3. abs.; con.	8. abs.; con.	13. con.; abs.
4. con.; abs.	9. con.; con.	14. con.; con.
5. con.; abs.	10. abs.; abs.	15. abs.; con.

PRONOUNS

EXERCISE 3, page 127

1. yourself	9. My
2. Everyone	10. those
3. our	11. Who
4. that	12. me
5. nobody	13. We
6. himself	14. who
7. their	15. These
8. many	

EXERCISE 4, page 128

	PRON.	ANTE.
1.	himself	Louis Braille
2.	it	accident
3.	that	school
4.	themselves	books
5.	who; him	pianist; Braille
6.	his	Braille

7. he; it
8. that
   he; his
   himself
   other
9. which
10. his
    who; themselves

man; vow
money
Braille; Braille;
Braille
people
system
Louis Braille
people

ADJECTIVES
EXERCISE 5, page 129

ADJ.	WORD(S) MODIFIED
1. long	journey
vast	deserts
2. Polo	brothers
Venetian	merchants
3. holy	oil
4. higher	peaks
any, other	mountains
5. correct	direction
6. That	trip
wondrous	places
7. grand	city
golden	statues
8. sandy	hills, valleys
no	food
9. summer	palace
eastern	city
10. historic	journey
three	years
11. foreign	official
Asian	empire
12. one	trip
Yunnan	province
13. traveling	official
keen, truthful	observer
14. incredible	tales
mysterious	China
15. curious	writer
famous	travels
16. first	record
Chinese	civilization
17. Some	descriptions
other	people
18. European	explorers
19. clear	It
courageous, resourceful	Marco
20. twenty-four	years

VERBS
EXERCISE 6, page 132

1. intr.		6. trans.
2. trans.		7. intr.
3. trans.		8. trans.
4. trans.		9. intr.
5. intr.		10. intr.

EXERCISE 7, page 132

VERB PHRASE	HELPING VERB(S)
1. will be	will
2. was transplanted	was
3. Must shout	Must
4. can remember	can
5. are debating	are
6. had helped	had
7. might have been sent	might have been
8. Does smile	Does
9. would win	would
10. is thinking	is

ADVERBS
EXERCISE 8, page 133

ADV.	WORD(S) MODIFIED
1. quickly; off	turned; v.
2. Completely	happy; adj.
3. later	was finished; v.
4. extremely	are talented; adj.
5. often	likes; v.
6. closer	Park; v.
7. ever	would get; v.
8. forward	push; v.
slowly	forward; adv.
9. Happily	ran; v.
10. almost	accidentally; adv.
accidentally	had found; v.
11. immediately	ran; v.
12. just	recently; adv.
recently	moved; v.
13. quite	fortunate; adj.
14. most	popular; adj.
15. Rather	formally; adv.
formally	introduced; v.

EXERCISE 9, page 134
(Answers will vary. Possible responses are given.)

1. amazingly	4. diligently
2. accidentally	5. now
3. nearby	

REVIEW EXERCISE 1
A., page 135

1. con.	6. con.; comp.
2. con.; comp.	7. abs.
3. con.; comp.	8. con.; coll.
4. con.; coll.	9. abs.
5. abs.	10. con.; comp.

B., page 135

1. l.v.	6. l.v.
2. a.v.; intr.	7. l.v.
3. a.v.; trans.	8. a.v.; trans.
4. a.v.; trans.	9. a.v.; intr.
5. a.v.; intr.	10. l.v.

C., page 136

PART OF SPEECH	WORD(S) MODIFIED
1. adv.	was dressed
2. adj.	crocodiles
3. adj.	hamburger
4. adv.	explained
5. adj.	wheel
6. adv.	Remind
7. adv.	wonderful
8. adj.	author
9. adj.	pilot
10. adv.	to look

D., page 136
(Answers will vary. Students will have fulfilled the assignment if responses include twenty-six entries following the guidelines provided.)

PREPOSITIONS
EXERCISE 10, page 138

PREPOSITION	OBJECT
1. to	Oregon
2. Over	Rainbow
3. for	years

4. During	1840s
of	baseball
5. on	table
6. in	afternoon
7. in	way
8. near	theater
9. with; to	him; me
10. in	vase
11. around	block
12. by	noon
13. against	odds
14. instead of	sweater
15. outside	solar system

EXERCISE 11, page 138

(Answers will vary. Students will have fulfilled the assignment if their work contains fifteen sentences using ten prepositional phrases with at least three prepositions.)

CONJUNCTIONS AND INTERJECTIONS
EXERCISE 12, page 140

	CONJUNCTION	CLASSIFICATION
1.	Even though	sub.
	and	coor.
2.	and	coor.
3.	not only, but also	corr.
4.	When	sub.
5.	Since	sub.
6.	Because	sub.
7.	but	coor.
8.	and	coor.
9.	or	coor.
10.	Although	sub.

EXERCISE 13, page 140

(Answers will vary. Students will have fulfilled the assignment if sentences properly use four interjections.)

DETERMINING PARTS OF SPEECH
EXERCISE 14, page 141

1. n.; pron.	6. adv.; prep.	11. pron.; n.
2. adj.; n.; adj.	7. adj.; pron.	12. intj.; adj.
3. adj.; v.	8. n.; adv.	13. n.; n.; prep.
4. n.; n.; prep.	9. n.; pron.	14. adv.; v.
5. conj.; v.	10. adv.; adj.	15. adj.; n.; v.

REVIEW EXERCISE 2
A., page 142

1. v.; adj.	8. conj.; adj.	15. v.; prep.
2. prep.; pron.	9. prep.; adj.	16. adv.; pron.
3. conj.; n.	10. prep.; prep.	17. pron.; n.
4. adj.; n.	11. n.; n.	18. v.; n.
5. n.; prep.	12. pron.; adj.	19. prep.; adj.
6. adv.; adj.	13. adj.; v.	20. n.; n.
7. pron.; conj.	14. adv.; adj.	

CHAPTER REVIEW
A., page 143

1. adj.	6. n.
2. pron.	7. n.
3. adj.	8. adj.
4. pron.	9. adj.
5. adj.	10. pron.

B., page 143

1. adj.; adj.	6. conj.	11. adv.
2. pron.; prep.	7. adj.	12. prep.
3. adj.; n.	8. n.	13. v.
4. adj.; prep.	9. conj.	14. pron.
5. conj.; v.	10. v.	15. adj.

C., page 144

(Answers will vary. Possible responses are given.)

1. I enjoyed both films.
2. The well is deep.
3. Whew, we made it after all.
4. Chris turned red at that remark.
5. Don't go unless they call.
6. Holly sat next to the vice president at the meeting.
7. Let the cat go outside.
8. We rested after the long climb.
9. Babe Ruth hit the pitch outside the park.
10. My father turned the car around.
11. Can you read that sign for me?
12. She said to take the pencil or the pen because either would do.
13. Butch not only delivered the papers, but he also fixed the window.
14. Please sign on the dotted line.
15. I like the people that moved in next door.

CHAPTER 11:
THE SENTENCE

SUBJECTS AND PREDICATES
EXERCISE 1, page 145

	COMPL. SUBJECT	COMPL. PREDICATE
1.	Who	was your favorite actor in that movie
2.	Jorge	arranged the grapes, apples, and oranges in a ceramic bowl
3.	George	threw back the covers of his bed
4.	Magda	noticed the blooming cherry trees in the park
5.	Which herbal tea	is the most healthful
6.	Francesca	Instead of going to the concert, studied for her Russian exam
7.	The tree boughs	drooped under the weight of the wet snow
8.	the frightened rabbit	Into the bushes, fled
9.	I	For recreation, practice yoga every other day
10.	A group of downtown merchants	protested the city's street repair plan
11.	Yori	recognized the constellation to the south
12.	Meeting at the library, many volunteers	prepared for the book sale
13.	The dress rehearsal for *Fiddler on the Roof*	will be after school tomorrow

14.	the cat	Is sleeping on the windowsill
15.	Lessons in breathing, floating, and kicking	were taught to the young swimmers
16.	Feeding on sunflower seeds every day, one gray squirrel	grew chubbier than the others
17.	The tired physician	leaned back in her chair for a short nap
18.	Blueberry bagels	are a popular breakfast item in our household
19.	Having read the *Joy Luck Club*, everyone	enjoyed seeing the film adaptation
20.	Anton	Did visit his grandparents in St. Petersburg

EXERCISE 2, page 146

	SUBJECT	VERB
1.	sister	did go
2.	All	were delivered
3.	dog	stretched
4.	awards	were presented
5.	Gregg	will play
6.	Elena	Did find
7.	Laura	ran
8.	Apples	spilled
9.	ship	sailed
10.	family	will return

COMPOUND SUBJECTS AND COMPOUND VERBS

EXERCISE 3, page 147

	SUBJECT	VERB
1.	Water	lapped; tickled
2.	coach; team	won; celebrated
3.	Snow; ice	threatened
4.	Anticipation; excitement	kept
5.	Each	studied; excelled
6.	Kazuo; Taro	flew; visited
7.	Tamara; Misha	speak
8.	plane; passengers	had been delayed
9.	plants; animals	live; thrive
10.	we	ate; played; danced

EXERCISE 4, page 148

(Answers will vary. Possible responses are given.)

1. Before going outside, Rena and Rinda put on their coats. (*s.*—Rena, Rinda; *v.*—put on)
2. The guests arrived on Thursday night and didn't leave until Monday. (*s.*—guests; *v.*—arrived, did leave)
3. Marta, Jamal, and Mark are learning how to play Go. (*s.*—Marta, Jamal, Mark; *v.*—are learning)
4. After cleaning the attic, Franklin sorted old photographs, called his sister, and invited her to dinner. (*s.*—Franklin; *v.*—sorted, called, invited)
5. When steamed and served with fresh lemon, broccoli and green beans taste crisp and zesty. (*s.*—broccoli, beans; *v.*—taste)

6. Last week, Bruce and Roberto played the saxophone in the open jazz competition. (*s.*—Bruce, Roberto; *v.*—played)
7. After the dress rehearsal, Miriam walked home, ate dinner, and practiced her lines one more time. (*s.*—Miriam; *v.*—walked, ate, practiced)
8. The young couple replastered, sanded, and painted the old ceilings. (*s.*—couple; *v.*—replastered, sanded, painted)
9. Amanda took the reins from Kevin and mounted the horse. (*s.*—Amanda; *v.*—took, mounted)
10. *David Copperfield, Bleak House,* and *Great Expectations* are great novels by Charles Dickens. (*s.*—*David Copperfield, Bleak House, Great Expectations*; *v.*—are)

FINDING THE SUBJECT OF A SENTENCE

EXERCISE 5, page 149

	SUBJECT	VERB
1.	<u>philanthropist</u>	<u>collected</u> <u>donated</u>
2.	<u>seagulls</u>; <u>ducks</u>	<u>were swooping</u>
3.	<u>herd</u>	<u>bathed</u> <u>played</u>
4.	(<u>you</u>)	<u>Turn</u> <u>follow</u>
5.	<u>printmaker</u>; <u>assistant</u>	<u>experimented</u>
6.	<u>Marla</u>; <u>Theresa</u>; <u>Jamie</u>	<u>met</u> <u>walked</u>
7.	<u>ferns</u>; <u>apples</u>	<u>carpeted</u>
8.	<u>Janet</u>	<u>steamed</u> <u>made</u>
9.	<u>Gregory</u>; <u>Margaret</u>	<u>registered</u>
10.	<u>seeds</u>; <u>millet</u>	<u>are</u>
11.	<u>musician</u>	<u>practiced</u> <u>started</u>
12.	<u>cat</u>	<u>paced</u> <u>looked</u>
13.	<u>disc jockey</u>	<u>opened</u> <u>closed</u>
14.	<u>Mr. Martínez</u>; <u>Ms. Chung</u>	<u>have earned</u> <u>were honored</u>
15.	<u>diner</u>; <u>newspaper stand</u>	<u>have closed</u>
16.	<u>paper</u>	<u>covered</u>
17.	<u>Whales</u>; <u>icebergs</u>	<u>are</u>
18.	<u>Alice</u>; <u>Anton</u>	<u>were hiding</u>
19.	<u>City hall</u>	<u>has been remodeled</u> <u>opens</u>
20.	<u>Felicia</u>	<u>stood</u> <u>watched</u>
21.	<u>record</u>; <u>service</u>	<u>earned</u>
22.	<u>peninsula</u>	<u>shimmers</u> <u>hosts</u>
23.	<u>group</u>	<u>attended</u> <u>voiced</u>
24.	<u>Peonies</u>	<u>grow</u>
25.	<u>birdhouses</u>; <u>feeders</u>	<u>were being built</u> <u>(were being) painted</u>

DIRECT OBJECTS AND INDIRECT OBJECTS

EXERCISE 6, page 151

1. granddaughter (i.o.); ring (d.o.)
2. scientists (d.o.); laboratory (d.o.)
3. cousins, me (i.o.); statue (d.o.)
4. cardinals (i.o.); seeds (d.o.)
5. her (i.o.); scholarship (d.o.)
6. us (i.o.); soup, salad, bread (d.o.)
7. elevator (d.o.)
8. us (i.o.); photos (d.o.)
9. sonatas, quartets, symphonies (d.o.)
10. time, skills (d.o.)
11. exhibit (d.o.)
12. Frank (i.o.); instructions (d.o.)
13. events (d.o.)
14. Bill (i.o.); term paper (d.o.)
15. us (i.o.); seats (d.o.)
16. apples (d.o.), pitcher (d.o.)
17. houses, farms (d.o.)
18. father (i.o.); card (d.o.)
19. roads (d.o.); us (d.o.)
20. invitation (d.o.)
21. me (i.o.); photographs (d.o.)
22. customer (i.o.); pairs, sweater (d.o.)
23. spirits (d.o.)
24. us (i.o.); performance (d.o.)
25. list (d.o.)

OBJECTIVE COMPLEMENTS

EXERCISE 7, page 153

1. green
2. amazing
3. sleek; sophisticated
4. fountain
5. treacherous
6. friend
7. president
8. Lara
9. fake
10. co-chair
11. Romeo; Juliet
12. clean
13. serious
14. surprise
15. sad

REVIEW EXERCISE

A., page 154

SUBJECT	VERB
1. they	meet
2. Joel; Sharon	are reading
3. Stories; plays	are
4. Yolanda	has read; does like
5. Ivan; he	agrees; does enjoy

B., page 154

1. flowers (d.o.)
2. fresh (obj. cmpt.)
3. abilities (d.o.)
4. company (i.o.)
5. beautiful (obj. cmpt.)
6. honey (d.o.)
7. prize (d.o.)
8. chef (i.o.)
9. green (obj. cmpt.)
10. closed (obj. cmpt.)

SUBJECT COMPLEMENTS

EXERCISE 8, page 155

	SUBJ. CMPT.	LINKING VERB
1.	one (p.n.)	is
2.	agriculture; tourism (p.n.)	are
3.	calm (p.a.)	became
4.	bitter; sour (p.a.)	can taste
5.	plant (p.n.)	is
6.	nervous (p.a.)	looked
7.	sensitive; powerful (p.a.)	are
8.	energetic; refreshed (p.a.)	felt
9.	source (p.n.)	is
10.	electric (p.a.)	was
11.	Julia; Eli (p.n.)	are
12.	mysterious (p.a.)	looked
13.	sticky (p.a.)	felt
14.	sweeter (p.a.)	smells
15.	maple (p.n.)	is
16.	relieved (p.a.)	looked
17.	hopeful (p.a.)	remained
18.	aromatic (p.a.)	are
19.	pianist (p.n.)	is
20.	raspy; dry (p.a.)	sounded

EXERCISE 9, page 156

(Answers will vary. Possible responses are given.)

1. soothing
2. a famous opera singer
3. confident, professional
4. a cabinetmaker
5. Schubert, Mozart
6. stark, dramatic
7. bland
8. McIntosh, Delicious
9. mournful
10. surprised, thrilled

CHAPTER REVIEW

A., page 157

SUBJECT	VERB
1. people	find
others	fall
2. bagpipes	are
3. player	fills
4. player	squeezes; forces
5. drones; chanter	are
6. Air	goes
7. player	can tune
8. rest	goes
9. chanter	has
10. musician	places

B., page 157

1. films (d.o.)
2. loaves (d.o.)
3. master (p.n.)
4. photographs (d.o.); wonderful (obj. cmpt.)
5. Sam (i.o.); mug (d.o.)
6. order (d.o.)
7. elegant, refined (p.a.)
8. hunter (p.n.)
9. poems (d.o.)
10. inflation (d.o.)
11. success (p.n.)
12. refreshed (p.a.)
13. books (d.o.)
14. athlete (p.n.)
15. concert (d.o.)

C., page 158

(Answers will vary. Students will have satisfactorily completed this exercise if the article has a title and includes at least fifteen sentences based on the notes that are given. At least one compound verb, one compound subject, one direct object, and one indirect object in the article should be underlined and labeled.)

CHAPTER 12: THE PHRASE

PREPOSITIONAL PHRASES

EXERCISE 1, page 159

	PREP.	OBJ. OF PREP.
1.	for	prom
2.	in	coat
3.	on	collie
4.	to	post office
5.	on; for	desk; project
6.	to	game
7.	through; in	hole; backpack
8.	with	felt
9.	over	shoulder
10.	above	door
11.	in	body
12.	on; with	car; steel wool
13.	in	forest
14.	near	Dutch oven
15.	after; of	shifting; gears
16.	around	block
17.	from	here
18.	over	bridge
19.	into	right field
20.	in	barrel

EXERCISE 2, page 160

(Answers will vary. Possible responses are given.)

1. Don't be alarmed by the dogs.
2. If we win, we are invited to Liseli's house for a celebration.
3. Have you ever gone swimming in a creek?
4. My brother has a blister on his hand where he grips the lawnmower handle.
5. I took this picture of a mongoose during my trip to India.
6. Have you any money with you?
7. We brought our own shovels for the trench-digging contest.
8. If Jody doesn't take the tapes to Mother, who will?
9. That bobsled run on the first hill looks awfully dangerous.
10. Lon bought a great used bicycle from the shop on Main Street.
11. I like to wear a sweater around the house.
12. We went to the airport and nearly got lost.
13. The Drapers had a great time at the performance.
14. Did you see U2 when they came to the arena?
15. Under the giant beech tree, Floyd sat by himself.
16. I packed a cheese sandwich for my lunch on the train.
17. The dog took a long nap in the shade of the elm tree.
18. My friends arrived in town last night.
19. A vegetable pizza is baking in the oven.
20. That wool sweater with the cable stitch is something I could make.

ADJECTIVE PHRASES AND ADVERB PHRASES

EXERCISE 3, page 161

	PHRASE	WORD MODIFIED
1.	for our two-night backpacking trip (adj.)	food
2.	from work (adj.)	vacation
3.	about our plans (adv.)	told
4.	since last month (adv.)	had been planning
5.	At home (adv.)	prepared
6.	except the water (adj.); into little plastic bags (adv.)	everything; went
7.	Instead of throwing them away (adv.)	bring
8.	in front of all that food (adv.)	Sitting
9.	with socks, sweaters, and the food (adv.)	loaded
10.	from his time (adv.); in the service (adj.)	had saved; time
11.	Unlike him (adj.)	I
12.	to the bottoms (adv.); of our backpacks (adj.)	tied; bottoms
13.	After a long hike (adv.)	reached
14.	until morning (adv.)	slept
15.	before sunrise (adv.)	awoke
16.	into the car (adv.)	loaded
17.	along the empty freeway (adv.)	drove
18.	in front of us (adj.); behind us (adj.)	car; car
19.	At last (adv.); at the trailhead parking lot (adv.)	arrived; arrived
20.	in the car (adv.)	did lock
21.	beside each other (adv.); for a while (adv.)	walked; walked
22.	across the first ridge (adj.)	way
23.	along the way (adv.)	rested
24.	next to me (adv.); at the morning sky (adv.)	sat; looked
25.	about a hiking trip (adj.)	thing

EXERCISE 4, page 162

(Answers will vary. Commend responses that give directions in a sensible order. Prepositional phrases should be identified.)

PARTICIPLES AND PARTICIPIAL PHRASES

EXERCISE 5, page 163

1. shingled
2. stewed
3. fading
4. Having showered; dismayed
5. spotted; endangered
6. fishing; broken
7. baked
8. spending
9. driving
10. polished
11. honking
12. wrinkled
13. having walked
14. Bagged; recycling
15. Running; crying

EXERCISE 6, page 164

PART. PHR.	WORD MODIFIED
1. given to him at birth	name
2. Born in Los Angeles in 1928	Pancho
3. Living in Southern California	he
4. competing at a high level without a coach	difficult
5. known for its speed and fierce attack	playing
6. Having turned professional in 1949	Pancho
7. Completing his final year as an amateur	he
8. winning the championship seven years in a row	he
9. playing on clay or on grass courts	he
10. Admired for his powerful serves	Pancho

GERUNDS AND GERUND PHRASES
EXERCISE 7, page 166

GER.	TYPE
1. Jogging	s.
2. flying	d.o.
3. marketing	o.p.
4. studying	s.
5. sliding	d.o.
6. sculpting	p.n.
7. Tracing	s.
8. purring	s.
9. cooking	o.p.
10. reading	p.n.

EXERCISE 8, page 166

GER. PHRASE	TYPE
1. going to the town library	o.p.
2. browsing in the stacks of books	p.n.
3. Going to the reference room	s.
4. trapping unwary researchers that way	d.o.
5. closing the library	o.p.

INFINITIVES AND INFINITIVE PHRASES
EXERCISE 9, page 167

1. to learn	4. to choose
2. to read	5. to talk; to vote
3. to govern	6. to dismiss
7. to dismiss	9. to add
8. To impeach	10. to propose

EXERCISE 10, page 168

INF. PHRASE	TYPE	WORD MODIFIED
1. to visit the Grand Ole Opry in Nashville	n.; d.o.	
2. to give your receipts to	adj.	person
3. to buy some of Lottie Walker's famous baked goods	adv.	went
4. to talk to us about the movie	n.; d.o.	
5. To drive in the Indy 500	n.; s.	
6. to listen to Duke Ellington play	adv.	walked
7. to get a crew cut	adv.	fun
8. to be leaving tomorrow	adv.	happy
9. to fit at his new desk	adv.	designed
10. to buy a poster for our bedroom	adj.	money

APPOSITIVES AND APPOSITIVE PHRASES
EXERCISE 11, page 169

APPOSITIVES	WORDS IDENTIFIED
1. ones	envelopes
2. teachers	Ms. Lin and Mr. Rinaldo
3. wood	pine
4. winner	project
5. runner	Jesse Owens
6. 6 Carlos Street	location
7. one	raincoat
8. expert	guest
9. specialty	soup
10. flower	carnation

EXERCISE 12, page 170

APP. PHR.	WORDS IDENTIFIED
1. our new dog	Shep
2. over two hundred people	Everyone
3. a former fighter pilot	stepfather
4. his company's cashier	sister
5. a novel called *The Life of a Sixteen-Year-Old*	book
6. my favorite vegetable	corn on the cob
7. the "Emerald Isle"	Ireland
8. the "planner"	brother
9. a lawn-furniture manufacturer	company
10. a posh tenplex	theater
11. a professor at Tufts University	uncle
12. the one with the crazy TV commercials	dealer
13. third period English	class
14. fifty geometry problems	homework
15. Sue's cousin	Sara

CHAPTER REVIEW
A., page 171

TYPE	WORD MODIFIED
1. adj. phr.	cup
2. adv. phr.	walked
3. adv. phr.	were covered
4. adv. phr.	kept
5. adj. phr.	view
6. adj. phr.	island
7. adv. phr.	completely
8. adj. phr.	those
9. adv. phr.	warm
10. adj. phr.	can

B., page 171

TYPE	FUNCTION
1. part. phr.	adj.
2. ger. phr.	d.o.
3. ger. phr.	o.p.
4. part. phr.	adj.
5. inf. phr.	d.o.
6. part. phr.	adj.
7. inf. phr.	p.n.
8. ger. phr.	s.
9. inf. phr.	d.o.
10. inf. phr.	s.
11. ger. phr.	o.p.

12. part. phr.   adj.
13. ger. phr.   d.o.
14. ger. phr.   o.p.
15. inf. phr.   adv.

C., page 172
(Answers will vary. Possible responses are given.)

1. The roads were jammed <u>because of the festival</u>.
2. My friend Peter is <u>from Belgium</u>.
3. Seeing the racehorses <u>leaping over us</u> was terrifying.
4. The sofa, <u>moved from its usual spot</u>, was constantly getting in the way.
5. We needed a rest after <u>replacing a flat tire</u> in the snow.
6. <u>Applying for a job</u> requires persistence.
7. I wanted <u>to taste</u> that before you threw it away.
8. I need a new hat <u>to wear</u> in the rain.
9. My wish was <u>to see Whitney Houston</u> live.
10. We gave Wanda, <u>one of my teammates</u>, a ride home.

CHAPTER 13:
THE CLAUSE

KINDS OF CLAUSES
EXERCISE 1, page 174

1. indep.	6. indep.	11. sub.	16. indep.
2. sub.	7. sub.	12. sub.	17. sub.
3. sub.	8. indep.	13. indep.	18. sub.
4. indep.	9. sub.	14. sub.	19. indep.
5. sub.	10. indep.	15. sub.	20. sub.

THE ADJECTIVE CLAUSE
EXERCISE 2, page 176

	ADJ. CL.	*REL. PRON./ ADV.*	*WORD MOD.*
1.	who enjoys swimming	who	Molly
2.	where thousands had died	where	battlefield
3.	which occurred in A.D. 79	which	eruption
4.	which my stepfather built	which	desk
5.	who had been exploring for twenty-five years	who	Howard Carter
6.	that he had made of the band's concert	that	tape
7.	where the kachina ceremony will be held	where	kiva
8.	when she watched the eclipse	when	evening
9.	[that] he saw last night	[that]	film
10.	[that, when] the choir rehearsed the Slovenian song	[that, when]	time

EXERCISE 3, page 176
(Answers will vary. Possible responses are given.)

1. The bus that was going to Cleveland departed from the station at noon.

2. Jacy used the red toothbrush that was hanging on the rack.
3. The door that Melvin opened led to the basement.
4. The baseball pitcher who pitched a no-hitter was elated.
5. Does the battery that you put in this flashlight still have a charge?
6. Hira, who is extremely tired, may sleep on the futon.
7. A large crowd gathered in the park where the hot-air balloons would land.
8. Fran must fix a flat tire on the bicycle that she borrowed from Janet.
9. Enrique walked quickly to the store where the sale was being held.
10. Joan enjoyed the stew that Addie Sue had prepared.

THE ADVERB CLAUSE
EXERCISE 4, page 178

	ADV. CL.	*WORDS MOD.*
1.	Although the work was not difficult	took
2.	unless there is below-zero weather	should run
3.	than anyone else at the table	slowly
4.	As Akoni's catamaran sped across the lake	darkened
5.	as long as you take proper care of it	may use
6.	than anyone had ever seen it before	deeper
7.	whenever we hear about a worthwhile film	go
8.	If we mail our orders in November	should receive
9.	While he was waiting for the bus	practiced
10.	because she had not tried them before	difficult
11.	as soon as you add the spices	ready
12.	Whenever her baby sister is asleep	works
13.	that I can't understand him	quickly
14.	than I am	better
15.	until our street became one enormous puddle	fell

EXERCISE 5, page 178
(Answers will vary. Possible responses are given.)

1. <u>Until a cold rain fell</u>, it was not a bitterly cold day.
2. The thread was worn <u>before the button fell off</u>.
3. The jacket was not warm enough <u>after the sun went down</u>.
4. She felt relieved <u>when the most difficult test was over</u>.
5. One Feather was in the first rank <u>while Young Bear wanted to make the team</u>.

THE NOUN CLAUSE

EXERCISE 6, page 179

1. d.o.; how an engine works
2. s.; Whichever piece Lawanda plays
3. p.n.; whether we should buy or rent snorkeling equipment
4. o.p.; whomever she asked for a job
5. p.n.; whatever my mother selected
6. d.o.; what is assigned to her
7. s.; Whoever was awarded the prize
8. i.o.; whoever is interested
9. o.p.; where construction blocked traffic
10. i.o.; whoever heckled him
11. s.; How much students practice
12. d.o.; whatever is on the menu
13. o.p.; whoever sits underneath it
14. p.n.; which of the keys had been stolen and replaced
15. i.o.; whoever seemed interested

EXERCISE 7, page 180

(Answers will vary. Possible responses are given.)

1. Put whichever chairs you prefer at the front of the stage.
2. Mr. Ramírez agreed to sell whatever wooden toys we made.
3. Whoever leaves the room last should switch off the lights.
4. That the home team usually wins pleases Ms. O'Toole greatly.
5. Mei Hua didn't know whether sandstone is a sedimentary rock.
6. I sent whoever was visiting my uncle Guido a map and directions.
7. Whichever plants are cacti need water only twice a month.
8. Nobody knows when the concept of zero was developed.
9. Mr. Hirata explained why the magnetic north pole differs from the geographic north pole.
10. The letter carrier will deliver whatever cards are addressed and stamped.

SENTENCE STRUCTURE

EXERCISE 8, page 181

1. simp.	5. cd.-cx.	9. cx.
2. comp.	6. cx.	10. cx.
3. cx.	7. comp.	
4. simp.	8. cd.-cx.	

SENTENCE PURPOSE

EXERCISE 9, page 183

1. dec.; period
2. inter.; question mark
3. dec.; period
4. dec.; period
5. imp.; exclamation point
6. inter.; question mark
7. excl.; exclamation point
8. dec.; period
9. dec.; period
10. inter.; question mark
11. excl.; exclamation point
12. inter.; question mark
13. imp.; period
14. excl.; exclamation point
15. inter.; question mark
16. dec.; period
17. inter.; question mark
18. imp.; period
19. imp.; period
20. excl.; exclamation point
21. imp.; exclamation point
22. dec.; period
23. dec.; period
24. inter.; question mark
25. imp.; period

CHAPTER REVIEW

A., page 185

1. indep. cl.
2. adj. cl.
3. n. cl.
4. adv. cl.
5. adv. cl.
6. n. cl.
7. adj. cl.
8. indep. cl.
9. n. cl.
10. adj. cl.

B., page 185

1. simp.; dec.
2. cd.-cx.; dec.
3. cx.; inter.
4. comp.; imp.
5. comp.; inter.
6. cx.; excl.
7. simp.; dec.
8. cx.; imp.
9. cx.; inter.
10. cd.-cx.; dec.

C., page 186

(Answers will vary. Possible responses are given.)

Today

I believe that having many different experiences is important. (noun cl.)

I dream of being a sports hero and a comedian and President.

I want to do the best and be the best that I can. (adj. cl.)

I fear that my life is boring.

Yesterday

I learned much when I watched fans at a football game. (adv. cl.)

When fans were booing a player who had dropped the ball, I stayed silent.

The people with louder voices didn't notice me.

But I dared them to do as well, working under such pressure.

Tomorrow

If I learn from my mistakes, I will succeed with my plans.

I will achieve what I want because I won't let critics bother me.

Listen to me, and watch what I do.

You will see me become stronger and better each year.

CHAPTER 14: AGREEMENT

SUBJECT-VERB AGREEMENT

EXERCISE 1, page 187

1. gallops
2. bloom
3. are shouting
4. announces
5. is practicing
6. slice
7. decide
8. hears
9. flex
10. is charging
11. tower
12. leap
13. are crumbling
14. hovers
15. is waiting
16. carry
17. boils
18. are uniting
19. dazzles
20. forgets

EXERCISE 2, page 188

1. are collecting
2. visit
3. covers
4. maneuvers
5. translates
6. is refinishing
7. alphabetizes
8. speak
9. has
10. are gathering
11. are performing
12. is totaling
13. play
14. collect
15. are shelving
16. marks
17. is throwing
18. is holding
19. are nesting
20. urge

INTERVENING PHRASES AND CLAUSES
EXERCISE 3, page 189

1. bakes	5. were	8. need
2. are filling	6. plant	9. make
3. is	7. is	10. support
4. are		

EXERCISE 4, page 190

1. has	6. is	11. matches
2. is	7. cover	12. is
3. is	8. (correct)	13. (correct)
4. are	9. is	14. describes
5. measures	10. has	15. (correct)

AGREEMENT WITH INDEFINITE PRONOUNS
EXERCISE 5, page 191

1. sound	14. attend
2. needs	15. hold
3. prepares	16. has
4. have	17. make
5. accepts	18. order
6. is	19. incorporates
7. is waving	20. vote
8. look	21. are experiencing
9. are	22. understands
10. run	23. is
11. offer	24. is
12. are	25. wants
13. are predicting	

THE COMPOUND SUBJECT
EXERCISE 6, page 193

1. was	10. are	19. bats
2. are	11. support	20. soften
3. see	12. schedule	21. grow
4. is	13. are learning	22. (correct)
5. (correct)	14. belong	23. sleep
6. look	15. is	24. are coming
7. are	16. grow	25. work
8. make	17. (correct)	
9. knows	18. make	

EXERCISE 7, page 194
(Answers will vary. Possible answers are given.)

1. Neither my mother nor my father know much about our family tree.
2. My father's parents and my mother's parents were of Irish background.
3. My maternal great-grandmother and great-grandfather married against the will of their families.
4. At the time neither her family nor his relations approved of the marriage between a Shawnee woman and an Irish immigrant.
5. Either her father or his parents publicly denounced them.

COLLECTIVE NOUNS
EXERCISE 8, page 195
(Answers will vary. Possible answers are given.)

1. a. The family vacations on the Maine coast every summer.
   b. The family enjoy various water sports.
2. a. The crowd surges forward as the politician approaches the podium.
   b. The crowd are shouting questions at the politician.
3. a. The wrestling team is undefeated this season.
   b. The wrestling team participate in other sports as well.
4. a. The choir performs six times during the year.
   b. The choir disagree about which piece should open the recital.
5. a. The committee is meeting on the school board's proposal.
   b. The committee are deadlocked on the issue.

REVIEW EXERCISE 1
A., page 196

1. study	5. shares	8. wants
2. are wearing	6. are	9. is
3. dedicates	7. assigns	10. is expecting
4. are		

B., page 196

1. is heading	5. reminds	8. grow
2. C	6. report	9. has
3. is dripping	7. are	10. C
4. provides		

OTHER PROBLEMS IN AGREEMENT
EXERCISE 9, page 199

1. are	6. has	11. reveals
2. has	7. is	12. is
3. are	8. was	13. are
4. is	9. is	14. aren't
5. is	10. has	15. have

EXERCISE 10, page 200

1. were	6. was	11. was
2. was	7. were	12. were
3. (correct)	8. was	13. tells
4. were	9. was	14. (correct)
5. were	10. were	15. owes

REVIEW EXERCISE 2
A., page 201

1. is	8. make	15. ranks
2. is	9. is	16. was
3. lead	10. are	17. were
4. need	11. observes	18. is
5. is	12. remains	19. is
6. are	13. have	20. are
7. are	14. What are	

B., page 202

1. have	6. leaves	11. are
2. has	7. (correct)	12. brings
3. have	8. was	13. is
4. (correct)	9. was	14. (correct)
5. sees	10. were	15. has

PRONOUN AGREEMENT
EXERCISE 11, page 205

1. his	5. its	9. his
2. its	6. itself	10. she
3. its	7. hers	11. itself
4. their	8. her	12. them

13. his or her   18. his   23. her
14. their   19. their   24. her
15. his   20. its   25. their
16. their   21. their
17. herself   22. her

EXERCISE 12, page 206

1. herself	6. his or her	11. her
2. (correct)	7. his	12. her
3. her	8. their	13. their
4. her	9. itself	14. her
5. he or she	10. their	15. their

CHAPTER REVIEW

A., page 207

1. is	8. C	15. participate
2. C	9. are	16. is
3. their	10. are	17. her
4. have	11. their	18. C
5. are	12. are	19. expects
6. his	13. is	20. their
7. is	14. C	

B., page 208

1. have existed	6. are	11. them
2. have used	7. is	12. were applying
3. (correct)	8. (correct)	13. (correct)
4. receives	9. creates	14. duplicate
5. appears	10. were made	15. is

C., page 208

(Answers will vary. A possible entry is given.)

Day 142, A.D. 2217

We reached the cold and rocky shore early this morning. The people who have greeted us seem as curious about us as we are about them. The inhabitants of this land live in tribes, and many of them are farmers. Some of the most intriguing finds have been many swords, helmets, and shields fashioned from iron.

CHAPTER 15: CORRECT PRONOUN USAGE

CASE OF PERSONAL PRONOUNS

EXERCISE 1, page 210

1. obj.	6. obj.	11. poss.
2. nom.	7. obj.	12. nom.
3. poss.	8. nom.	13. nom.
4. poss.	9. poss.	14. nom.
5. poss.	10. obj.	15. poss.

THE NOMINATIVE CASE

EXERCISE 2, page 212

1. I
2. He
3. (correct)
4. she
5. They

EXERCISE 3, page 212

1. she
2. we
3. he
4. he
5. We

THE OBJECTIVE CASE

EXERCISE 4, page 214

1. me	6. us	11. him	16. her
2. them	7. them	12. them	17. him
3. him	8. me	13. me	18. us
4. her	9. him	14. her	19. them
5. him	10. us	15. me	20. me

THE POSSESSIVE CASE

EXERCISE 5, page 216

(Answers may vary. Possible responses are given.)

1. my	6. yours
2. hers	7. Our
3. your	8. its
4. his	9. Their
5. her	10. mine

EXERCISE 6, page 216

1. them
2. Phil's
3. yours
4. Their
5. (correct)

SPECIAL PRONOUN PROBLEMS

EXERCISE 7, page 218

1. he	6. me	11. me	16. they
2. her	7. she	12. he	17. she
3. I	8. I	13. them	18. he
4. her	9. she	14. he	19. me
5. them	10. she	15. I	20. her

WHO *AND* WHOM

EXERCISE 8, page 220

1. whom	8. who	15. whoever
2. whoever	9. who	16. whom
3. Who	10. whom	17. whomever
4. who	11. who	18. Who
5. whom	12. whom	19. whom
6. who	13. who	20. who
7. who	14. whom	

CHAPTER REVIEW

A., page 221

1. whom	6. us	11. I
2. I	7. He	12. I
3. I	8. C	13. they
4. I	9. C	14. C
5. he	10. he	15. C

B., page 221

1. His	6. I
2. I	7. whom
3. who	8. they
4. me; her	9. I
5. I	10. you

C., page 222

(Answers will vary. The exercise will be completed successfully if students include fifteen sentences correctly using pronouns as prescribed by the instructions.)

CHAPTER 16:
CLEAR REFERENCE

AMBIGUOUS REFERENCE
EXERCISE 1, page 224
(Answers will vary. Possible responses are given.)

1. I think the fact that my cousin Freda writes poems and stories is quite admirable.
2. By speaking clearly and to the point, the mayoral candidate should show up his opponents.
3. C
4. Holding a concert at the beach on the same night as the bowling tournament caused some confusion.
5. The corporal reported to the lieutenant that the lieutenant's patrol was missing.
6. Receiving a card from my brother and a book from my aunt while I had the flu made me happy.
7. C
8. Lauren's pony kept right on going after it bumped into the fence.
9. The cast was pleased that more than two hundred people came to see the play on opening night.
10. Helen called Marie while Marie was out.
11. The pirates thought that digging a deep hole and hiding the chest in it would protect their treasure.
12. The dark sky and flash of lightning meant a storm was on the way.
13. Julio noticed that Ken was wearing Julio's Western boots.
14. Because Lenore spoke so well in public, our English teacher chose her to represent the class.
15. Wapi later regretted having ridden the roller coaster on an empty stomach.
16. Although they flew right into the trees, the birds weren't hurt.
17. We are proud of our college's excellent science department and beautiful campus.
18. Before leaving for Brazil, Cesar told Juan that Juan's cousin was going with him.
19. Until it was covered with clouds, Kai observed the moon through the telescope
20. The fire chief asked Stan to bring his own hat.

WEAK AND INDEFINITE REFERENCE
EXERCISE 2, page 225
(Answers will vary. Possible responses are given.)

1. Katie enjoys in-line skating with her new skates and says skating is her favorite sport.
2. Duc is an excellent pianist, but he has never owned a piano.
3. Some fish are saltwater fish. They require salt water to live.
4. In politics, politicians don't always know all the answers.
5. The index does not list a page reference for information about the Canadian flag.
6. A documentary on the wolf will be presented on television.
7. The editorial section of the newspaper discusses the forthcoming presidential election.
8. C
9. We stopped at the record store at the mall, but we didn't buy any records.
10. Ms. Wilson said that the museum was worth visiting, but the tour would take more than two hours.
11. We were late for school because we missed the bus this morning.
12. Most people prefer truthful leaders, but some people think truthfulness is not important.
13. C
14. Only a sharp eye is able to find a well-camouflaged female bird.
15. In many Japanese restaurants, tea is served with each meal.
16. C
17. Kari is very shy, but she doesn't show her shyness when she's with our family.
18. Each time Marvin hears country music, he wants to become a country singer.
19. The aerobics class worked so hard that the exercise made them breathless.
20. Early motion pictures show the actors moving and walking very fast.
21. My father is an art teacher at the high school, but I know nothing about art.
22. On Thursday, Sari spent an hour at the library, but she didn't find any books.
23. Al is interested in stamp collecting, so he wants to learn all he can about stamps.
24. Derek enjoys his career in architecture, so he measures carefully before he draws.
25. Clay and Jody entered the chess tournament, but Clay didn't win one game.

CHAPTER REVIEW
A., page 227
(Answers will vary. Possible responses are given.)

1. Ben wondered if Sam knew what Sam looked like up on stage.
2. Writing me a letter and sending it overnight will make me happy.
3. Blanche ran to the water's edge, dived in, and had a terrific swim.
4. Having Sergio climb those three trees while using the correct ropes and handholds will be good practice for him.
5. Dad's congratulating me and giving me a slap on the back made me feel good.
6. The polls showed the challenger cutting into the incumbent's popularity.
7. When we saw the canoes coming our way and our friends waving, we waved back.
8. The dish crashed to the floor and broke.
9. My brother likes my cousin, even though my cousin's always borrowing my brother's jacket.
10. Having to pay ten dollars for the two packages and four dollars for lunch made her grumpy.

B., page 227
(Answers will vary. Possible responses are given.)

1. These statistics indicate that inflation was lower last year.
2. My brothers traveled to see the famous band in concert during the band's final appearance in this country.

3. Mixing the molasses with the honey might make the recipe too sweet.
   Try not to mix the molasses with the honey because the honey might make the recipe too sweet.
4. Pietro caught the pass, took three fast steps toward the basket, and, at the last minute, made the shot one-handed.
5. When Hetty kept singing that song over and over, sentimental tears filled her mother's eyes.
6. C
7. The team put on their uniforms and then went out to play the game.
8. In Pop's old store, there would always be bargains.
9. Serena was very pleased when she noticed Lorenzo was applauding more than anyone else.
10. The egg exploded when it landed on the sidewalk.

C., page 228

(Answers will vary. Students will have satisfactorily completed the assignment if they include time, place, characters, and plot and demonstrate an adequate knowledge of correct pronoun reference).

CHAPTER 17: CORRECT USE OF VERBS

REGULAR VERBS
EXERCISE 1, page 229

1. played	7. celebrated	14. painting
2. burned *or* burnt	8. listed	15. retiring
	9. finished	16. developed
3. walked	10. used	17. imagined
4. watching	11. phoned	18. stapling
5. expecting	12. paying	19. attacked
6. prejudiced	13. risked	20. asked

IRREGULAR VERBS
EXERCISE 2, page 233

1. sung	6. forgotten	11. built
2. frozen	7. drew	12. came
3. made	8. ran	13. rang
4. bought	9. went	14. sent
5. burst	10. stood	15. ate

EXERCISE 3, page 234
1. given
2. (*correct*)
3. took
4. knew
5. become

LIE AND LAY
EXERCISE 4, page 235

1. lying	6. lay	11. lies
2. laid	7. lying	12. lay
3. lies	8. laid	13. laid
4. lain	9. laid	14. lay
5. laying	10. lay	15. lying

EXERCISE 5, page 236

1. lying	6. lay
2. C	7. lies
3. laid	8. lain
4. lying	9. laid
5. lain	10. C

SIT AND SET AND RISE AND RAISE
EXERCISE 6, page 237

1. sat	8. sat	15. rose
2. risen	9. C	16. set
3. rising	10. Set	17. risen
4. setting	11. sat	18. sat
5. set	12. raised	19. C
6. rising	13. raise	20. sitting
7. raised	14. set	

VERB TENSE
EXERCISE 7, page 240

1. past perf.	8. pres. perf.	15. fut.
2. past	9. past	16. past
3. past	10. past	17. pres. perf.
4. past	11. fut. perf.	18. pres. perf.
5. pres.	12. pres. perf.	19. fut. perf.
6. past perf.	13. pres.	20. pres.
7. past	14. pres.	

EXERCISE 8, page 241
1. Pamela has been completing a five-hundred piece jigsaw puzzle.
2. Jason will build a wooden bird feeder as a present for Mr. Petner.
3. The rings-and-jewelry set included seed beads, wire, and directions.
4. After a long bus ride from Phoenix, the reggae band will be arriving in town.
5. Peter Jacobson has played music on the harpsichord for five years.
6. The bank on Main Street will have an automatic teller machine with a Braille keypad.
7. The class had been talking about a special show featuring sea turtles at the museum.
8. By the end of her trip to Germany, Eliza will have traveled to Berlin and several other cities.
9. I was reading about a small, powerful microscope for examining objects indoors and outdoors.
10. Atlanta, Georgia, is planning to hold the Summer Olympic Games in 1996.

SPECIAL PROBLEMS IN THE USE OF TENSES
EXERCISE 9, page 243

1. did exist	8. cost	15. had lived
2. were released	9. released	16. sat
3. began	10. crossed	17. was organized
4. set	11. had died	18. has replaced
5. had scored	12. wrote	19. won
6. served	13. had been	20. ended
7. has become	14. rode	

EXERCISE 10, page 245
1. Having arrived early
2. to read
3. to have underestimated
4. Having explained

5. to buy
6. Having inherited
7. Serving
8. to establish
9. to prepare
10. Having listened
11. Beginning
12. to have bought
13. to get
14. Having been
15. closing
16. to dance
17. Having participated
18. Having lost
19. to have sung
20. to identify
21. to have been
22. Comparing
23. Having discovered
24. to have cooked
25. to have been

ACTIVE VOICE AND PASSIVE VOICE
EXERCISE 11, page 247

1. pass.	6. pass.
2. act.	7. act.
3. act.	8. pass.
4. pass.	9. act.
5. pass.	10. pass.

EXERCISE 12, page 248
(Answers may vary. Possible responses are given.)

1. Lugosi was rescuing an injured soldier; but during the rescue mission, an explosion hurled Lugosi into the air.
2. His head's hitting a rock on the ground caused the concussion.
3. Other famous men suffered serious wounds on the battlefield.
4. Ernest Hemingway endured twelve operations after bullets and shell fragments caused him serious wounds.
5. The famous author was driving an ambulance in Italy during World War I when he received the injuries.
6. In a 1571 battle against the Turks, a cannon ball permanently disabled the left hand of Miguel de Cervantes, the author of *Don Quixote*.
7. During World War II, shrapnel hit the chest of François Mitterrand, a future president of France.
8. Mitterrand had barely recovered from his wounds when enemy forces took him prisoner.
9. Jean Renoir's mother convinced doctors not to amputate her son's leg.
10. A bullet had broken the French artist's leg in a World War I battle.

MOOD
EXERCISE 13, page 249

1. were	8. be	15. be elected
2. were	9. weren't	16. were
3. were	10. mail	17. were
4. were	11. were	18. C
5. C	12. consider	19. were
6. lock	13. C	20. were
7. be	14. were	

CHAPTER REVIEW
A., page 251

1. known	6. sitting
2. (*correct*)	7. rise
3. written	8. Graduating
4. had said	9. will have been sitting
5. are	10. sit

B., page 251

1. Living	9. will have leaped *or* leapt
2. spend	10. thought
3. to steer	11. takes
4. were	12. They use their sharp claws
5. known	13. is
6. dived	14. (*correct*)
7. were	15. want
8. to escape	

C., page 252
(Answers will vary. The exercise will be satisfactorily completed if students write a descriptive message to a friend. Five past forms and five past participle forms of the irregular verbs in the chart on pages 231–233 should be used correctly in the message.)

CHAPTER 18:
CORRECT USE OF MODIFIERS

USES OF MODIFIERS
EXERCISE 1, page 253

1. confidently	10. realistically	19. diligently
2. proud	11. carefully	20. loudly
3. promptly	12. desperately	21. noisy
4. sincerely	13. immediately	22. hungrily
5. light	14. briskly	23. quickly
6. curious	15. restless	24. nervously
7. enthusiastically	16. loudly	25. harsh
8. grumpily	17. blindly	
9. cheerful	18. efficient	

SIX TROUBLESOME MODIFIERS
EXERCISE 2, page 255

1. slowly	5. well	9. good
2. well	6. slowly	10. slowly
3. bad	7. well	
4. badly	8. bad	

EXERCISE 3, page 256

1. well	5. bad	9. slowly
2. C	6. well	10. C
3. badly	7. bad	
4. slowly	8. good	

COMPARISON OF MODIFIERS
EXERCISE 4, page 258

1. thicker, thickest
2. more clearly, most clearly
3. more thankful, most thankful
4. grayer, grayest
5. littler, littlest *or* more little, most little
6. more silently, most silently
7. more rapid, most rapid
8. more elegant, most elegant
9. more dramatically, most dramatically
10. longer, longest
11. more elaborate, most elaborate
12. more, most

13. narrower, narrowest
14. greener, greenest
15. more fully, most fully
16. more precious, most precious
17. more successful, most successful
18. happier, happiest
19. more likely, most likely
20. more warmly, most warmly
21. worse, worst
22. more ill, most ill
23. tinier, tiniest
24. more completely, most completely
25. better, best

USES OF COMPARATIVE AND SUPERLATIVE FORMS

EXERCISE 5, page 260

1. anyone else
2. most
3. least
4. best
5. calmest
6. anyone else
7. quickly; more quickly; most quickly
8. juicier
9. most
10. worst
11. less
12. more
13. anyone else
14. worse
15. less

CHAPTER REVIEW

A., page 261

1. any other
2. steadily
3. most
4. thoughtfully
5. easier
6. bad
7. loveliest
8. anywhere else
9. most wonderful
10. anyone else
11. hotter
12. bad
13. most
14. deepest
15. carefully

B., page 262

1. famous
2. widely
3. best
4. rough
5. brightly
6. quickly
7. well
8. badly
9. anything else
10. C
11. best
12. most
13. partly
14. less
15. dramatic

C., page 262

(Answers will vary. Students should correctly use both comparative and superlative forms of modifiers in ten sentences.)

CHAPTER 19:
PLACEMENT OF MODIFIERS

MISPLACED MODIFIERS

EXERCISE 1, page 263

(Answers may vary. Possible responses are given.)

1. On the way home from the hospital, Fran talked about the illness she had had.
2. Harold saw your dog Spike digging a hole with his front paws.
3. My neighbor who writes children's books has a parakeet.
4. Eating our picnic lunch, we watched the clouds drift by.
5. I remember I was involved in antipollution activities during the *Exxon Valdez* oil spill.
6. Please put this vase on the table near the piano.
7. For his family, he made a loaf of bread that has raisins in it.
8. After class, the teacher asked the two students to report to the office.
9. Lori said we would go to Santa Fe after Hanukkah.
10. For my cat, we found a veterinarian who specializes in skin diseases.
11. Please tell the man I need the firewood on Monday.
12. I can see your shoes hidden under the table.
13. They learned she was a tour guide at the museum.
14. In the garden, a woodchuck dug a hole that is unbelievably deep.
15. We hired a tutor for my sister who needs extra help in math.

DANGLING MODIFIERS

EXERCISE 2, page 265

(Answers may vary. Possible responses are given.)

1. While fishing, I caught these trout.
2. Flying out of Cuba, we could see the coast of Florida.
3. Because Denise performed beautifully, her reward was loud applause.
4. Extremely talented, the performer's strengths are singing and dancing.
5. After Henri had read the book, the movie version seemed dull to him.
6. Missing Tanya, the neighbors were filled with sadness.
7. To do well in school, you need to work hard.
8. While we were looking for our friends, the concert began.
9. Having read about Samoa, I made my travel plans.
10. Because Chaka and Solomon were watching the children play, their afternoon slipped by.
11. When training for a race, runners find that sturdy shoes are helpful.
12. To learn about current events, read newspapers.
13. A storm began suddenly while the Outdoors Club members were hiking in the mountains.
14. Their laughter could be heard as they told jokes and funny stories.
15. Because the wall is built of bricks, its strength is guaranteed.

CHAPTER REVIEW

A., page 267

(Answers may vary. Possible responses are given.)

1. In one legend, gray birds that arrive at that mosque turn white within forty days.
2. For her brother, Gwen made a costume covered with stars and stripes.
3. Please give the woman in the blue dress a program.
4. Above the sofa, Roberto hung the picture painted by Alicia.
5. At a school assembly, the firefighters spoke about the need for courage.

6. Paolo, also an Italian bicycle racer, cheered when Claudio crossed the finish line.

7. These vases that are made of marble will hold several flowers.

8. For his cousin, he built a boat made from recycled materials.

9. At the post office, Gerry bought stamps that show rock-and-roll musicians performing.

10. I want to ask Rosemary to have lunch with me when she finishes her work.

B., page 268

(Answers may vary. Possible responses are given.)

1. While I was watching the movie, my brother came home.

2. Begun as an experiment, the business that Joe's dad started is now successful.

3. While they were looking at old photographs, memories came back to them.

4. To find the meanings of words, use a dictionary.

5. Having chopped the vegetables, Tamara was ready to serve the meal.

6. While I was listening to Erik's description, vivid pictures came to my mind.

7. Anxious to begin the play, the actors on the stage were filled with tension.

8. By taking another helping of salad, John filled his plate.

9. He became prouder as he thought about past victories.

10. My face turned bright red because I had forgotten the poem I had memorized.

C., page 268

(Answers will vary. Possible responses are given.)

1. Maybe the ship came <u>from outer space</u>, and maybe not.

2. What I remember is seeing a large silver dish <u>that made strange noises</u>.

3. <u>Flashing its lights</u>, it was seen <u>cruising over the treetops</u> in the next block.

4. <u>Having spotted it in the night sky</u>, I ran to get my brother Raphael.

5. <u>To try to describe what I saw</u>, I drew a picture.

6. <u>Feeling curious and adventurous</u>, Raphael said, "Let's go outside to see if we can find it!"

7. <u>Hidden behind a grove of trees</u> in the park, the silver dish lay on the ground.

8. <u>Scattering birds and small animals</u>, it suddenly rose into the sky as we watched.

9. The part <u>that really startled me</u> was that it appeared to move on its own, <u>without any engine</u>.

10. I'll never know whether I was more surprised <u>because it hovered in one spot</u> or because it made such odd noises.

CHAPTER 20:
A GLOSSARY OF USAGE

ADAPT, ADOPT / BEING AS, BEING THAT
EXERCISE 1, page 270

1. as far as	6. were	11. adapted
2. illusion	7. as fast as	12. because
3. alumna	8. alumni	13. meet
4. number	9. number	14. illusions
5. adopt	10. allusions	15. Because

CREDIBLE / LIKE, AS, AS IF
EXERCISE 2, page 272

1. notorious	6. notorious
2. implied	7. emigrate
3. famous	8. as
4. suggest	9. inferred
5. immigrants	10. credulous

EXERCISE 3, page 272

	INCORRECT	*CORRECT*
1.	shows	show
2.	credulous	credible
3.	notorious	famous
4.	(*correct*)	
5.	like	as

NAUSEATED, NAUSEOUS / WHO, WHICH, THAT
EXERCISE 4, page 274

1. have	6. from	11. persecuted
2. nor	7. that	12. nauseous
3. nauseated	8. than	13. prosecute
4. somewhat	9. That	14. that
5. have	10. then	15. or

THE DOUBLE NEGATIVE
EXERCISE 5, page 275

1. any	6. could
2. any	7. anything
3. has	8. ever
4. ever	9. anyone
5. any	10. any

EXERCISE 6, page 276

(Some answers may vary. Possible responses are given.)

	INCORRECT	*CORRECT*
1.	no	any
2.	none	any
3.	no	any
4.	never	ever
5.	couldn't	could
6.	never	ever
7.	nothing	anything
8.	no	any
9.	could not	could
10.	no	any

A., page 277

(Some answers may vary. Possible responses are given.)

INCORRECT	CORRECT
1. illusions	allusions
2. live at	live
3. no	any
4. off	from
5. like	as if
6. adopted	adapted
7. famous	notorious
8. persecuted	prosecuted
9. then	than
10. inferred	implied
11. or	nor
12. had not	had
13. That there	That
14. like	as if
15. which	who *or* that
16. credulous	creditable *or* credible
17. alumnae	alumni
18. would of	would have
19. some	somewhat
20. nauseous	nauseated
21. all the farther	as far as
22. nothing	anything
23. is	are
24. off of	from
25. amount	number

B., page 278

INCORRECT	CORRECT
1. prosecution	persecution
2. nor	or
3. (*correct*)	
4. must of	must have
5. implied	inferred

C., page 278

(Answers will vary. The exercise will be satisfactorily completed if the students write an article using correctly at least ten of the expressions listed.)

CHAPTER 21: CAPITAL LETTERS

PLACES AND PEOPLE

EXERCISE 1, page 280

1. Irish Sea; Ireland; England
2. Mount Kilimanjaro
3. Budapest; Danube River
4. Dead Sea
5. Baffin Island
6. Mesa Verde National Park; Colorado
7. Portugal
8. Suzuki; West
9. Los Angeles County
10. Langley Road

EXERCISE 2, page 280

1. Kurt Vonnegut; Indianapolis, Indiana
2. Fifty-eighth Street
3. Mount Whitney
4. Persian Gulf
5. Big Bend National Park; Texas; Alabama
6. Albany; Providence; Northeast
7. Colorado River; Gulf of California
8. Sequoia National Park
9. (*correct*)
10. Vietnam; Laos; Southeast Asia

SCHOOL SUBJECTS, FIRST WORDS, PROPER ADJECTIVES

EXERCISE 3, page 282

1. Brazilian	11. Oh
2. O	12. Ukrainian
3. Algebra I	13. Latin
4. If; What	14. Julia's; At
5. Just; Alaskan	15. Belgian; Swedish
6. social studies	16. English
7. The; Russian	17. Roman
8. 100-watt	18. Have
9. I	19. Mexican; Spanish
10. Italian	20. Have

GROUPS, ORGANIZATIONS, AND RELIGIONS

EXERCISE 4, page 284

1. a.	5. b.	8. a.
2. a.	6. a.	9. a.
3. a.	7. b.	10. b.
4. a.		

EXERCISE 5, page 284

1. Boy Scouts of America
2. Bureau of the Census
3. (*correct*)
4. League of Women Voters
5. Charlotte Hornets
6. Silva Brothers Florists
7. New York Philharmonic
8. Leonardo's
9. Christmas Eve; New Testament
10. Hudson's Bay Company

REVIEW EXERCISE

A., page 285

1. b.	5. a.	8. a.
2. b.	6. b.	9. b.
3. a.	7. a.	10. a.
4. b.		

B., page 285

(Answers may vary. Possible responses are given.)

1. I visited Aunt Margaret for a week.
2. Sean bought this at T-Shirts to Go.
3. Ms. Perez got her degree at Princeton University.
4. In religion class we studied Judaism and Hinduism.
5. Are you Portuguese or Spanish?
6. The conference is in Portland, Oregon.
7. We are flying to Saudi Arabia next month.
8. Her address is 1405 South Maple Street.

9. Many wonderful recipes come from the South.
10. There were pictures of the Falkland Islands on the news last night.
11. Was there a fire in the Eagle National Forest?
12. The photograph was of El Capitan in the southern mountain range.
13. What was your grade in geography?
14. I like eating French pastries.
15. There was a hurricane in the Gulf of Mexico.

OBJECTS, EVENTS, AND AWARDS

EXERCISE 6, page 287

1. Washington Monument
2. *Salem Express*
3. Macintosh Quadra
4. Boston Tea Party
5. Memorial Day; Veterans Day
6. Pulitzer Prize
7. April Fools' Day
8. Jazz Age
9. Venus
10. *Dona Paz; Victor*
11. Medal of Honor
12. French Revolution; American Revolution
13. Boeing
14. New York World's Fair
15. Alpha Centauri
16. Enlightenment
17. Wednesday; Saturn
18. Special Olympics
19. Verbatim
20. Pegasus

TITLES

EXERCISE 7, page 290

1. *Wealth Without Risk*
2. *National Geographic*
3. mom
4. "Blues at Dawn"
5. *The Wall Street Journal*
6. *L. A. Law*
7. *The Man from the Other Side*
8. (*correct*)
9. *Entertainment Tonight*
10. Piano Concerto No. 2
11. Declaration of Independence
12. *Star Wars; Return of the Jedi; The Empire Strikes Back*
13. *From Beirut to Jerusalem*
14. (*correct*)
15. *Des Moines Register*
16. Strategic Arms Reduction Treaty
17. Uncle
18. "The Fatalist"
19. Justice
20. *Birthday Party for Lala and Tudi*

CHAPTER REVIEW

A., page 291

1. Italy; Mount Etna
2. Eddie; Rosie's Fajitas
3. Parliament; Great Britain
4. father; Did; IRS
5. Rodin's *The Thinker*
6. *The Norton Anthology of American Literature*
7. Tylenol; Stop & Shop; Saturday
8. Great Wall of China; Thanksgiving
9. Uncle Virgil's; *The Rubáiyát;* Omar Khayyám
10. Spanish; Friday; Beacon Street

B., page 291

1. Caribbean Sea; north
2. United States; September; Independence Day
3. Spain

4. Among
5. (*correct*)
6. Lenca
7. Mestizos; Indian
8. President Rafael Leonardo Callejas Romero
9. National Congress
10. Central American Common Market

C., page 292

(Answers will vary. Students should write at least fifteen sentences and should follow rules of capitalization in this chapter.)

CHAPTER 22: PUNCTUATION

END MARKS

EXERCISE 1, page 294

1. That's amazing!
2. Frank asked, "What's for dinner?"
3. Whose pile of laundry is this?
4. Sarah asked why we don't visit her more often.
5. Last night Herb balanced his checkbook.
6. Are you going to Yolanda's graduation party?
7. This town enforces its speed limits.
8. Run, Chester, run!
9. Nancy put on her jacket and sped away.
10. How is Mr. Joseph's condition today?
11. Don't you dare tell!
12. Did you hear Laura say, "Thank you"?
13. Miriam yelled, "Yikes!"
14. Will you just forget it!
15. We asked Rudy about his job interview.

ABBREVIATIONS

EXERCISE 2, page 295

1. (*correct*)
2. Dr. Ivan Ivanovich
3. 12 oz
4. 2 kg
5. (*correct*)
6. Luisa Gutierrez, D.D.S.
7. (*correct*)
8. A.D. 1237
9. Little Rock, Ark.
10. State Police Assn.

REVIEW EXERCISE

A., page 296

1. The 10-kg package was mistakenly shipped to Fargo, N. Dak.
2. Could you see the lunar eclipse after 10:00 P.M.?
3. After programming the VCR, we taped our favorite PBS program.
4. You should talk to J. B. Lancer, Jr.!
5. Why do we have to leave so early for the Howard St. station?
6. Ace Co., Bravo Assn., and Competent Corp. were cited as up-and-coming U.S. businesses.
7. Did Mr. Elliott really have an interview with the FBI at 8 A.M.?
8. According to the story I heard, Constance caught a 6-lb trout.
9. B. J. Chee ran the 50-yd dash in under six seconds! (*or* .)
10. The telegram was addressed to Ms. Sally V. Shelton.
11. We've recently moved to 138 Ash St., Portland, Oreg.
12. The FCC issued new rules for cordless telephones.

13. Dr. Fisk said the baby weighed exactly 3 kg at birth.
14. The tournament was is Madison, Wis., at the university.
15. No! Come back later! (*or* .)

B., page 296
(Answers will vary. Students will satisfactorily complete this exercise by using all three types of end marks to correctly punctuate each of the fifteen sentences.)

COMMAS IN A SERIES
EXERCISE 3, page 298

1. On Tuesday, Martin misplaced his books, his wallet(,) and his watch.
2. Every morning, Darren enjoys oatmeal, wheat toast with peanut butter, and juice.
3. Before chewing the couch, the puppy ate my slippers, my gloves(,) and my brother's hat.
4. C
5. Marco and Marie named their four children Martha, Mary, Marsha(,) and Sam.
6. C
7. The decorations committee hung balloons in the cafeteria, in the gymnasium(,) and above the lockers in the hall.
8. Franklin, Yoshi(,) and James are my three best friends.
9. C
10. Many of the plays performed at this theater were written by well-known playwrights such as Wasserstein, Shepard, Stoppard(,) and Mamet.
11. Exercising three times a week, eating a balanced diet(,) and drinking water will bring you good health and well-being.
12. They say she is a dedicated, experienced(,) and energetic leader.
13. C
14. Nobody knew who the contest winners were, when they had been selected(,) or when they would be announced.
15. My little brother's favorite foods are rice, macaroni and cheese, and bananas.
16. The critic hailed the author's latest mystery novel as "Cunning, suspenseful, wicked(,) and wonderful!"
17. Go to the corner of West End and 76th Street, turn right onto 76th, and walk three blocks to our apartment.
18. C
19. Thank you for the lovely evening, the delicious dinner(,) and the exquisite dessert.
20. Choose any of these colors: green, yellow, blue, red.

COMMAS WITH COMPOUND INDEPENDENT CLAUSES
EXERCISE 4, page 299

1. Yukio explained her reasoning, but Charles wasn't listening.
2. The oranges were large and plump, yet the apples looked more refreshing.
3. I called the box office, but the concert was already sold-out.
4. For Thanksgiving we placed extra chairs around the table, and everyone felt too crowded.
5. C
6. The sculptor did not want the clay to dry, so he covered it with a damp cloth.
7. Everyone was offered a choice of rice or potatoes, yet many people asked for couscous.
8. In the attic, Emily found old letters stored in shoeboxes, and she didn't know what to do with them.
9. Jack usually enjoys ice skating or skiing, but the weather is too warm this winter.
10. Jamal studied the photographer's technique, for he wanted to learn the process.
11. Bob suggests that I plant marigolds around the garden, or pests will invade the tomatoes again.
12. C
13. C
14. Adele and Ted enjoyed the book, but they didn't want to see the film adaptation.
15. Chad was so tired after two hours of shoveling, yet he cleared his neighbor's sidewalk, too.
16. C
17. Odessa is a person's name(,) and it is also the name of a place.
18. Is the Coliseum in Paris(,) or is it in Rome?
19. Only yesterday Tamisha left on the train, yet Phoebe says it feels like weeks have passed since her visit.
20. The tutor says my work is improving, but she thinks I need better study habits.
21. We looked at the Roman drawings and sculptures, and then we stood in line to see the Hermitage collection.
22. Finally, the children took a nap, but they didn't stay asleep for long.
23. C
24. The store is only open Monday through Friday, but the owner will schedule special appointments for Saturday.
25. Ivan and Ben spoke different languages, yet that was not a barrier to their friendship.

COMMAS WITH NONESSENTIAL ELEMENTS
EXERCISE 5, page 302

1. n.e.; Monday, which is my sister's birthday, is the first day of school.
2. n.e.; The dog covered with fleas would not stop scratching.
3. n.e.; Alice Munro, who is my favorite author, lives in Canada.
4. e.
5. n.e.; The trout, which had been caught by Uncle Bob, was served for dinner.
6. n.e.; After Alisha meets with her accountant, who is our neighbor, she'll file her income taxes.
7. n.e.; This park, known for its orchid hybrids, has a new groundskeeper.
8. e.
9. e.
10. e.
11. n.e.; Hector washed his little brother's face, which was covered with peanut butter.
12. n.e.; The staff, excited by the promise of a holiday, worked even harder.
13. e.
14. n.e.; Jasmine, who had excelled in science, has been nominated for a Pulitzer Prize.

15. n.e.; Brussels sprouts, which look like tiny cabbages, flourish in cool weather.
16. n.e.; The writer, frustrated by the neighbor's loud stereo, did not complete the manuscript on time.
17. e.
18. n.e.; My older brother's children, who are named Stefan and Tasha, make me feel young and energetic.
19. n.e.; Natalie Beltoya, whose parents are from Belorussia, fluently speaks three languages.
20. n.e.; We were amazed that the architect, pressured by construction deadlines, completed the building on schedule.

COMMAS WITH INTRODUCTORY ELEMENTS
EXERCISE 6, page 303
1. No, we do not wish to order dinner yet.
2. Covered completely with dust, the bookshelves, cabinets, and chairs revealed neglect.
3. Hey, did you hear Juanita's good news?
4. Scratching at the carpet, the old dog tried to bury an imaginary bone.
5. On the shelf behind the tureen, I've hidden Hank's birthday gift.
6. When they called, I met them at the airport.
7. C
8. Holding the model in her hands, Maxine dreamed about planes she'd fly someday.
9. Until the rooster crowed, not even the cows mooed.
10. Maybe, but let's see what happens next.
11. In a low valley under a pine tree, they finally pitched their tent for the night.
12. Swinging their arms, they happily walked along the beach.
13. C
14. Quick as ever, the juggler tossed a dozen tomatoes into the air and caught them.
15. Dressed in brightly colored costumes, we danced in the streets at Mardi Gras.
16. Yes, I got your message.
17. Anxious that David was late, Luis called David's parents.
18. After the guests had left and throughout the rest of the night, they washed dishes.
19. Well, I don't really know what to think.
20. Having sung the aria, the diva left the stage.
21. At the base of the mountain in a cave, a reclusive miner keeps his home.
22. Thanking all of the volunteers, the radio announcer finally ended the fund drive.
23. Man, is it ever cold out here!
24. Okay, but let's meet at the movies anyway.
25. After she found her tickets, Amelia put on her coat, locked the door, and hurried to the airport.

COMMAS WITH OTHER SENTENCE INTERRUPTERS
EXERCISE 7, page 306
1. Your cat, by the way, seems quite friendly.
2. In fact, Victor flew to Moscow last week.
3. Carole, have you seen the book that I was reading?
4. Frank's mother, an engineer, likes the household to run smoothly.
5. C
6. Parsley, the best-growing plant in our garden, is often nibbled to its roots by birds.

7. C
8. I wonder, Tom, when you'll bring us good news.
9. That shade of purple looks terrific on you, Latisha.
10. Nevertheless, Jeff Brown, the class president, asked for a vote recount.
11. For example, I study after school with Jamal, a math tutor.
12. Naturally, our Labrador Chester didn't feel well after eating that many treats.
13. Marjoram tastes sweet, yet slightly pungent, when simmered with tomatoes.
14. My brother said, "Nick, you need a haircut."
15. C

OTHER USES OF COMMAS
EXERCISE 8, page 307
1. After writing the letter, she signed it, "Sincerely yours, Odessa."
2. Isn't that Frank Sinatra, Jr., singing that song?
3. My dental appointment is on Monday, February 13, 1995.
4. He lived at 110 Cactus Court, Albuquerque, New Mexico, for ten years.
5. Louis, Sr., visited Louis, Jr., in Farmington last week.
6. C
7. The invitation read, "Dear Alani, Please join us for dinner on Saturday."
8. C
9. Arthur Lewitt, Jr., has the same birthday as I do.
10. A young researcher made the discovery at the University of Rochester in Rochester, New York.
11. Seattle, Washington, is still considered a desirable place to live.
12. I heard that Sharon arrives next Saturday, March 14.
13. Her business cards read, "Tina Nakai, J.D."
14. He wrote a letter of complaint to 22 Stratosphere Lane, Jupiter.
15. We arrived late at the graduation of Helen Carter, M.D., Ph.D.
16. On August 21, 1994, we had a wonderful picnic.
17. Our son Victor Reynosa, Jr., was born on March 17, 1977.
18. The sign above the doorbell read, "Janet Washington, M.D."
19. The nearest fruit market is located at Highway 30, Racine, Wisconsin.
20. C
21. C
22. Our next meeting will be at 30 Cedar Street, Davenport, IA 52803.
23. Did you know that Derek Maddox, Jr., made the varsity team?
24. C
25. After turning right at the corner, you'll find 500 Main Street, Eugene, Oregon, on your left.

CHAPTER REVIEW
A., page 309
1. Quick, throw the ball to Hank!
2. C
3. Charles Washington, Jr., my neighbor, lives down the block at 7500 Paulina Street.
4. She signed the letter, "Yours truly, Veronica I. Smith."

5. Were you born on March 1, 1977, or March 7, 1971?
6. The talk show guest, who was a famous athlete, announced his retirement and spoke of his future plans.
7. Karen ironed her shirts, pants, and skirts; and Misha, her husband, folded the last load of clothes from the dryer.
8. Hot and sweaty and tired, they pulled dozens of weeds from the garden.
9. Taking the bench, the judge looked at the jury, cleared his throat, and asked if they had reached a decision yet.
10. Do you know if FBI stands for Federal Bureau of Investigation?
11. She wondered if Stefan heard her, but he didn't.
12. C
13. Ms. Schumann, a promising scientist, prefers to spend her holidays reading adventure novels.
14. Running ahead of the other dogs, the boxer caught the stick that I threw.
15. Well, you could have fooled me. (*or* !)
16. Eager to be at sea, the young men volunteered their services aboard the steamer *Argos*, and they leave tomorrow.
17. For example, if Jim, Jr., comes home early, you can bet soccer practice will be cancelled.
18. Energetic and strong, the gymnast who was last year's silver medalist won the gold.
19. Henry, before those muffins burn, take the pan out of the oven.
20. C

B., page 310

[1] Bonsai, small, ornamental trees, are grown in low, shallow pots. [2] Very slow growers, they are shaped over a long period of time. [3] For example, one of the bonsai, a dwarf maple, was over fifty years old. (*or* !) [4] Some bonsai, if cared for tenderly and properly, live to be hundreds of years old. [5] C

C., page 310

(Answers will vary. This exercise will be successfully completed if students write a brief report of ten sentences containing a clear explanation of the game idea and answering the five questions asked in the exercise. A variety of end marks should be included, and sentences should be punctuated correctly.)

CHAPTER 23: PUNCTUATION

SEMICOLONS AND COLONS
EXERCISE 1, page 312

1. Sandi decided to cut her hair; it had started to hang over her eyes.
2. The coach called a time out, and he told the team which play to run; then he sent in a substitute for Kramer.
3. Donna is no longer on the cheerleading squad; instead, she stays after school to catch up on her classwork.
4. We rarely buy bread anymore; we have been making it ourselves at home.

5. Paquito put on an apron, hot mitt, and chef's hat; then he asked us if we wanted red, orange, or green peppers in our omelettes.
6. (*correct*)
7. When you arrive at Camp Winnebago, be sure you have brought the following items: towels, shampoo, insect repellent, rain gear.
8. The burglar seemed to know exactly where the alarm system was; how he knew is still a mystery.
9. Feeling tired, I took a hot bath; I had a light snack; and I went to bed early.
10. Dorotea was staying up all night: Her government term paper was due the next day, and she had barely begun to work on it.
11. I am certainly much too clumsy to perform in public; nevertheless, I enjoy dancing so much that I had to audition.
12. "Your oral reports will be graded on the following points: organization, clarity, completeness, and audience interest," the teacher informed us.
13. Mr. Mori said: "Ladies and gentlemen, we are here tonight to honor a distinguished co-worker and longtime friend."
14. Mario invited me to his house; he's got a new math game for his computer.
15. Kibbe loved his home; however, he also wanted to visit new places.

OTHER MARKS OF PUNCTUATION
(Answers will vary. Possible responses are given.)
EXERCISE 2, page 314

1. Vincente considered. "Well, . . . I'm not so sure about that."
2. I said that what was mine was hers—not that I had much to give.
3. The author made one character say, "Yipes! . . . Now I have nowhere to go!"
4. The first people in North America—the people Columbus called "Indians"—lived on both coasts and everywhere in between.
5. The new rule is—you probably already heard this—everyone has to wear a white shirt.
6. Dr. Seuss (his real name is Theodor Geisel) has also written under the pseudonym Theo. LeSieg.
7. The quarterback—I can't think of his name—threw six touchdown passes.
8. Senator John Glenn (Ohio) first gained fame as an astronaut.
9. "I think I hear . . . something in the basement," Tal whispered.
10. Some of the other students—Lula and Esteban, for example—have already begun their third project.

UNDERLINING (ITALICS)
EXERCISE 3, page 316

1. It's rare for a motion picture to win the Academy Awards for Best Actor, Best Director, and Best Picture, as <u>Ben-Hur</u> did, isn't it?
2. My favorite Frank Sinatra album is <u>Strangers in the Night</u>. What's yours?

3. When I want to watch reruns of old television shows, I always look for <u>Bewitched</u>.
4. The musical play <u>The Wiz</u> was based on the film <u>The Wizard of Oz</u>.
5. My neighbor Bill Neibergall is a photographer for the <u>Des Moines Register</u>.
6. The first steam-powered ship to cross the Atlantic was the <u>Savannah</u> in 1818.
7. <u>Fraktur</u> is the German name for the fancy typeface that somewhat resembles Gothic script.
8. My dad and I watch <u>60 Minutes</u> together, but we skip the commercials.
9. I plan to read <u>The Age of Innocence</u> before I see the film version.
10. There's a reproduction of Trumbull's painting <u>The Declaration of Independence</u> in my civics book.
11. The world's largest submarine, the USS <u>Triton</u>, is over thirty years old.
12. What have you learned about Michael Collins, one of the astronauts on <u>Apollo 11</u>?
13. Can you tell me the difference between <u>whoever</u> and <u>whomever</u>?
14. This book, <u>What Color is Your Parachute</u>, is about getting a job, but it also helps you learn about yourself.
15. The movie <u>Beethoven's 2nd</u> uses a <u>2</u>, not <u>two</u>, in the title.
16. If you were famous, would you rather have your picture on the cover of <u>Life</u> or the <u>National Enquirer</u>?
17. If you think the play <u>Cats</u> is popular, you should know that <u>A Chorus Line</u> had more than six thousand performances on Broadway.
18. I heard someone joke, "Either you liked the movie <u>Wayne's World</u>, or you're an adult."
19. Although it has no rhyme, Homer's epic <u>Iliad</u> is written in verse.
20. My three-year-old sister Uma called her clay blob <u>Penguins at School</u>.

APOSTROPHES

EXERCISE 4, page 318

1. the toy soldiers' march
2. Charles's hat
3. whose lunch box
4. their house
5. Stone & Rock Co.'s office
6. someone's guess
7. Sheila's and Bill's drawings
8. the cats' food
9. someone else's plans
10. the geese's honks

QUOTATION MARKS

EXERCISE 5, page 321

1. Our teacher read us Bacon's essay entitled "Gardens."
2. "Coach," said Adrian, "please explain your strategy once more."
3. The referee yelled, "Break it up!"
4. The firefighter came on the radio and asked, "Where's the fire?"
5. Did Luna really say, "The dog ate my homework"?
6. "Stop asking questions!" yelled Ms. Stamos, exasperated.
7. The artist said, "The sunshine is beautiful; it is reflecting magically off the water."
8. "Let me come," begged Joe, "and I will help with the work—and the food!"
9. "Surely you are joking! (or,)" said the principal sternly.
10. Kichi said, "My favorite poem is 'My Mother Pieced Quilts.'"

EXERCISE 6, page 322

1. The announcer said, "I asked Nancy Kerrigan, 'What's the most important skill for a skater?'"
2. The title of this story, "The Moustache," really interests me.
3. "Bill, come here quickly!" yelled Magda. "The birds are building a nest."
4. The pirate growled, "Tell me the secret!"
5. Did your grandmother always say to you, "Eat your vegetables!"?
6. Buying a lottery ticket, Ken said, "Sometimes you win"; but I say, "not very often."
7. Tammy's best friend Hilda asked her, "What did you mean when you told Guido, 'Hilda's getting to be a pest'?"
8. "This is serious," said our mother, "and I will not tolerate any joking."
9. The census taker inquired, "What's your name?"
10. "Who's your daddy?" asked the little girl.
11. "Was it James Hurst," asked Matti, "who wrote 'The Scarlet Ibis'?"
12. What would you think about a song called "Don't Worry. Be Happy"?
13. (correct)
14. "Well," drawled the impersonator, "who do you think I'm supposed to be?"
15. "Excuse me," she said, clearing her throat. "Is there any chance you could supply us with menus?"

CHAPTER REVIEW

A., page 323

1. Is that James's or the Joneses' rake?
2. (correct)
3. Does everyone's lunch have a raw vegetable and a piece of fruit?
4. The Bureau of Indian Affairs' news release was important.
5. "I'd say that's a good week's work! (or ,)" she estimated.
6. "So . . . ," the questioner began, "you say you did not arrive until 7:12 P.M.? (or.)"
7. To decide whether to write <u>a</u> or <u>an</u>, think about the way in which the next word is spelled and pronounced.
8. The artistry of <u>The Persistence of Memory</u> is not only in the painting but also in the name.
9. At a museum we saw a life-size replica of the <u>Spirit of St. Louis</u>, Charles (nicknamed "Lucky") Lindbergh's famous airplane.
10. I always fall asleep just before <u>Entertainment Tonight</u> comes on the television.
11. How many <u>u</u>'s are in <u>vacuum</u>?
12. I'm sure you've heard the overture to Rossini's opera <u>William Tell</u>.

13. My stepbrother's car needs new upholstery and new tires.
14. The women's locker room looks just like the men's.
15. "Hey!" Corinne asked. "Why did that man name his boat <u>Elvis</u>?"

B., page 323

(Answers will vary. Possible responses are given.)

[1] James S. Coleman, a sociologist from the University of Chicago, chaired the Panel on Youth, which wrote this book. [2] The panel asked itself an enormous question: How are young people brought into adulthood in the U. S.? [3] In an agricultural society, children work with adults: One can see examples in <u>Little House on the Prairie</u> and many other books. [4] With industrialization, children have become more isolated from family; for work, being done mostly in the city, is isolated from family life. [5] Children do not learn as often the work of their parents; children's futures are no longer determined by their parents' occupations. [6] A striking fact of modern times is that, besides their parents and teachers, children have less contact with adults. [7] The group feels age segregation had its benefits: It freed adults to work more efficiently and protected children from dangerous workplaces.

[8] However, children now have less opportunity to learn what adult life is like; adults have less opportunity to enjoy being with children; there is less sharing of activities, less discussion, and, consequently, less understanding between generations. [9] The panel suggested that the costs of age segregation (see chart) are higher than the benefits. [10] They suggest we ask if schools are the only places in which young people can learn to work: Their answer is no.

C., page 324

(Answers will vary. Sentences should include an answer to each of the *5W-How?* questions. Students should correctly capitalize and punctuate their sentences.)

CHAPTER 24: SPELLING

THE DICTIONARY

EXERCISE 1, page 326

1. mo-men-tar-i-ly
2. potatoes
3. (Answers may vary. Possible answers include: 1. a unit of weight; 2. to beat to a pulp or powder; 3. an enclosure for animals.)
4. defied
5. An allusion by Theodore Roosevelt to the man with the muck rake in Bunyan's *Pilgrim's Progress*.

EXERCISE 2, page 326

1. theatre
2. valour
3. blameable
4. encyclopaedia
5. synagog

SPELLING RULES

EXERCISE 3, page 327

1. receipt	10. their	19. belief
2. piece	11. fierce	20. priest
3. grief	12. friend	21. counterfeit
4. handkerchief	13. feign	22. weird
5. niece	14. chief	23. shield
6. pier	15. beige	24. reindeer
7. field	16. ceiling	25. yield
8. seized	17. neither	
9. brief	18. sleigh	

EXERCISE 4, page 328

1. friend; proceeded	4. interceded	8. acceded
2. receded; view	5. ancient	9. believe
3. scientists	6. (*correct*)	10. (*correct*)
	7. preceding	

PREFIXES AND SUFFIXES

EXERCISE 5, page 330

1. undo	8. immortal	15. advantageous
2. kindness	9. surely	16. disappoint
3. remake	10. illogical	17. finally
4. becoming	11. openness	18 stored
5. unintentional	12. noticeable	19. immaterial
6. wisely	13. merrily	20. densely
7. mileage	14. rediscover	

EXERCISE 6, page 330

1. mediator	8. heaviness	15. happily
2. judgment	9. timeless	16. moderation
3. bravely	10. really	17. interestingly
4. careful	11. dosage	18. notable
5. activity	12. busily	19. hopefully
6. practically	13. cleanliness	20. fascination
7. outrageous	14. continuous	

EXERCISE 7, page 331

1. cooking	8. fairest	15. warily
2. funnier	9. shipped	16. hopping
3. batted	10. putting	17. paired
4. marrying	11. smarter	18. reddest
5. treated	12. coyness	19. sledding
6. nearest	13. sunnier	20. carried
7. joyful	14. sailing	

EXERCISE 8, page 332

1. Ordinarily	8. destroyed	14. nearer
2. mysterious	9. extraordinarily	15. tried
3. beginnings	10. sailed	16. claimed
4. various	11. portrayed; glorious	17. monasteries
5. beautiful	12. created	18. trapped
6. happiness	13. (*correct*)	19. terrifying
7. occurred		20. denying

PLURALS OF NOUNS

EXERCISE 9, page 333

1. waltzes	10. turtles	19. inventors
2. valleys	11. lunches	20. dishes
3. dimes	12. wishes	21. dresses
4. Forsters	13. ideas	22. Rosses
5. mountains	14. boxes	23. fezes
6. songs	15. Katzes	24. benefits
7. radishes	16. dancers	25. marches
8. glasses	17. Morrisons	
9. Martinezes	18. watches	

EXERCISE 10, page 334

1. wolves	8. knives	14. monkeys
2. Tuesdays	9. lives	15. chiefs
3. essays	10. pennies	16. Hardys
4. carafes	11. laundries	17. babies
5. trophies	12. lamps	18. reefs
6. Kellys	13. wharves	19. journeys
7. enemies	*or* wharfs	20. follies

EXERCISE 11, page 335

1. igloos	5. cellos	9. hairdos
2. lassos	6. lice	10. runners-up
3. sopranos	7. children	
4. radios	8. fathers-in-law	

EXERCISE 12, page 336

1. studios	5. photos	9. solos
2. Passersby	6. sopranos	10. tornadoes
3. concertos	7. sisters-in-law	*or* tornados
4. heroes	8. disc jockeys	

EXERCISE 13, page 336

(Answers will vary. Satisfactory answers will use the following plural forms.)

1. lookers-on	4. mosquitoes	6. burritos
2. feet	*or* mosquitos	7. pueblos
3. pianos	5. echoes	8. geese

9. halos *or* halos	15. altos	21. sopranos
10. two-year-olds	16. barrios	22. heroes
11. cameos	17. torpedoes	23. runners up
12. teeth	18. firefighters	24. bookshelves
13. tomatoes	19. women	25. zeros
14. brothers-in-law	20. vetoes	*or* zeroes

CHAPTER REVIEW

A., page 337

1. relief	8. courageous	15. keys
2. reindeer	9. timeless	16. Santiagos
3. succeed	10. magnifying	17. coral reefs
4. underrated	11. useful	18. lives
5. dosage	12. coolest	19. ceremonies
6. merrily	13. batter	20. echoes
7. seceded	14. ranches	

B., page 338

1. believe; men	6. mysteries
2. occurred; scaled	7. nearing
3. beginning; tried	8. achievement
4. succeeded	9. carefully
5. receive	10. risks

C., page 338

(Answers will vary. A satisfactory answer will have two spelling rules from the chapter with examples, exercises, and answers.)

ANSWER KEY: *Assessment Booklet*

CHAPTER 10:
PARTS OF SPEECH

DIAGNOSTIC TEST, page 1
A.

1. conj.	6. v.	11. v.
2. adv.	7. intj.	12. adv.
3. pron.	8. n.	13. conj.
4. prep.	9. pron.	14. n.
5. adj.	10. pron.	15. prep.

B.

(Answers may vary. Possible responses are given.)

16. <u>Washington</u> is the capital of our country.
    Have you eaten <u>Washington</u> apples?
17. Is that the <u>mail</u> on the table?
    Please <u>mail</u> the letter.
18. Search <u>inside</u> the house.
    Dad said we should stay <u>inside</u> today.
19. <u>Terrific</u>! I've always wanted to see that film.
    That's a <u>terrific</u> watch.
20. Rita <u>liked</u> tomatoes.
    No other hockey player is <u>like</u> John.

POSTTEST, page 2
A.

1. v.	6. pron.	11. conj.
2. pron.	7. intj.	12. adj.
3. adj.	8. n.	13. adv.
4. conj.	9. adv.	14. n.
5. prep.	10. prep.	15. v.

B.

(Answers may vary. Possible responses are given.)

16. What are you giving him for <u>Christmas</u>?
    The choir sang <u>Christmas</u> carols.
17. <u>No</u>, you may not!
    Why is there <u>no</u> answer?
18. The <u>cross</u> man frowned at the suggestion.
    <u>Cross</u> the street at the light.
19. You know that Sam is always going to tell
    that <u>joke</u>.
    Why are they always <u>joking</u>?
20. The horse jumped <u>over</u> the fence.
    We were happy when that exam was <u>over</u>.

CHAPTER 11:
THE SENTENCE

DIAGNOSTIC TEST, page 3
A.

1. v.	6. i.o.	11. obj. c.
2. s.	7. p.n.	12. i.o.
3. p.a.	8. obj. c.	13. p.a.
4. d.o.	9. s.	14. v.
5. p.a.	10. d.o.	15. p.n.

B.

16. Several, I; have researched
17. they; have
18. leaves; are
19. sprouts; Do grow
20. (you); Harvest, enjoy

POSTTEST, page 4
A.

1. i.o.	6. d.o.	11. obj. c.
2. p.a.	7. p.n.	12. obj. c.
3. p.n.	8. d.o.	13. d.o.
4. s.	9. v.	14. i.o.
5. s.	10. p.a.	15. p.n.

B.

16. you; Do prefer
17. some; are
18. you, friends; Have seen
19. (you); Go, see
20. photographs; are

CHAPTER 12:
THE PHRASE

DIAGNOSTIC TEST, page 5
A.

1. adv. phr.; lives	6. app. phr.; Vikings
2. adj. phr.; group	7. adv. phr.; whipped
3. adj. phr.; papers	8. adv. phr.; put
4. app. phr.; Renard	9. adj. phr.; winner
5. adv. phr; borrowed	10. app. phr.; tortilla

B.

11. part. phr.; adj.	16. ger.phr.; s.
12. ger. phr.; o.p.	17. ger. phr.; d.o.
13. inf. phr.; adv.	18. inf. phr.; p.n.
14. ger. phr.; s.	19. part phr.; adj.
15. inf. phr.; adj.	20. part. phr.; adj.

POSTTEST, page 6
A.

1. adv. phr.; lives	6. adj. phr.; nation
2. app. phr.; Chickadees	7. adv. phr.; floated
3. adj. phr.; books	8. adv. phr.; Hide
4. adv. phr.; caddies	9. app. phr.; attic
5. app. phr.; drill	10. adj. phr.; monk

B.

11. part. phr.; adj.	16. ger.phr.; s.
12. inf. phr.; adv.	17. part. phr.; adj.
13. part. phr.; adj.	18. ger. phr.; s.
14. part. phr.; adj.	19. inf. phr.; d.o.
15. inf. phr.; adv.	20. ger. phr.; o.p.

CHAPTER 13:
THE CLAUSE

DIAGNOSTIC TEST, page 7

A.

1. n. cl.
2. adj. cl.
3. adv. cl.
4. n. cl.
5. indep. cl.
6. adj. cl.
7. indep. cl.
8. adv. cl.
9. adj. cl.
10. adv. cl.

B.

11. comp.; dec.
12. cx.; dec.
13. simp.; dec.
14. cx.; inter.
15. simp.; imp.
16. cd.-cx.; dec.
17. cx.; inter.
18. cd.-cx.; dec.
19. simp.; excl.
20. simp.; imp.

POSTTEST, page 8

A.

1. adj. cl.
2. indep. cl.
3. adj. cl.
4. n. cl.
5. adv. cl.
6. adj. cl.
7. indep. cl.
8. n. cl.
9. adv. cl.
10. adv. cl.

B.

11. cx.; imp.
12. simp.; dec.
13. cx.; dec.
14. cx.; inter.
15. cd.-cx.; dec.
16. simp.; excl.
17. cx.; dec.
18. simp.; imp.
19. cd.-cx.; dec.
20. comp.; inter.

CHAPTER 14:
AGREEMENT

DIAGNOSTIC TEST, page 9

A.

1. is
2. make
3. is
4. roosts
5. blocks
6. make
7. have
8. need
9. works
10. contains
11. belong
12. receive
13. has passed
14. Where are

B.

15. I believe this generation and the next one should meet more of their energy needs with wind power.
16. Fossil fuels, such as coal and oil, are still our main energy sources.
17. When a home or a business burns fossil fuels for its energy needs, harmful gases are released.
18. Wind power, however, is one of those energy sources that do not harm the environment.
19. Wind power is also better than fossil fuels because it will never run out.
20. (*correct*)

POSTTEST, page 10

A.

1. help
2. is
3. stay
4. makes
5. is
6. teaches

7. is coming
8. wants
9. support
10. What's
11. have caused
12. has increased
13. are
14. becomes

B.

15. The United States bought the rights to the canal from the French and paid $40 million for them.
16. Both the Atlantic and Pacific sides of the canal have a series of three locks.
17. Either ships or a barge can carry its cargo through the locks.
18. (*correct*)
19. Each of the countries stated its requirements in the new agreement.
20. By December 31, 1999, Panama will take back full control of its canal.

CHAPTER 15:
CORRECT PRONOUN USAGE

DIAGNOSTIC TEST, page 11

A.

1. I
2. she
3. their
4. who
5. she
6. whom
7. She
8. him
9. their
10. Who
11. whoever; me
12. Our
13. he
14. them
15. she

B.

16. Whom—Who
17. me—I
18. him—he
19. (*correct*)
20. (*correct*)

POSTTEST, page 12

A.

1. he
2. me
3. him
4. whoever
5. their
6. their
7. he
8. they
9. us
10. Whom
11. who
12. Who
13. we
14. he
15. I

B.

16. myself—me
17. we—us
18. they—their
19. (*correct*)
20. her—she

CHAPTER 16:
CLEAR REFERENCE

DIAGNOSTIC TEST, page 13

A.

(Answers will vary. Possible responses are given.)

1. We noticed a dent in the side of the boat after it hit the dock.
2. Mariana made Luisa promise to wear Mariana's red dress.
3. Because the staging was spectacular and the acting was magnificent, the audience cheered.

4. Peter asked the optician if Peter needed new glasses.
5. The glove was burned by the time Sam took it off the radiator.
6. That computer store demonstrates new software products.
7. The hot day and long hike tired us.
8. During the conference, the minister asked the secretary of state to review the minister's report.
9. Your sister is a terrific baker, but I wonder how she gets her bread to have such great crust.
10. On most other planets the air is not breathable.
11. When Hector climbed to the top of the tree and swung from a branch, his friend got nervous.
12. When dropped on the rocks, the marbles shattered.
13. During football games the fans can be extremely enthusiastic.
14. He bored his listeners by speaking for thirty minutes without saying anything new.
15. Switzerland has great skiing.

B.

(Answers will vary. Possible responses are given.)
16. Those two brothers are always trying something adventurous.
17. Entering the dark cave at night with only one flashlight made Lok apprehensive.
18. "Some caves have a lot of bats," Hsu whispered bravely.
19. Hsu and Lok saw plenty of giant limestone formations but no bats, although the boys thought they heard them.
20. That they only stayed in the cave for an hour and were soon back home in their warm, well-lit living room made Lok happy.

POSTTEST, page 14
A.

(Answers may vary. Possible responses are given.)
1. Some films present a fairly realistic view of the Old West.
2. Eating well and exercising every day helps Wong stay fit.
3. After it hit the tree, the golf ball bounced twenty feet.
4. That cruise ship has three swimming pools and four restaurants.
5. I hadn't heard from my brother in over a year, so I opened his letter as soon as the mail had been delivered.
6. As Ted and Roland left the city, Ted said that he would return.
7. I've heard that the Prado Museum in Madrid has some of the world's greatest paintings.
8. Two months after the doctors put a cast on Robin's leg, the cast came off.
9. More people shop in malls than ever before.
10. Which island has the best beach?
11. By marching all day and moving at a brisk pace, the troop from Ohio arrived first.
12. We piled the wood in the fireplace and then lit a fire.
13. Several magazines featured the new president.

14. Every time Claudio saw the engines racing toward a fire with all their sirens blasting, he wished that he could be a firefighter.
15. Cleaning the attic and then practicing their speeches kept Deena and Babette busy all afternoon.

B.

(Answers will vary. Possible responses are given.)
16. "But these instruction books," said Ed, "say the tricks are easy to perform."
17. When Mickey laughed and said, "I think you had better stick to making milk and doughnuts disappear," Ed got angry.
18. Ever since Ed had seen the Great Renfew performing magic on stage, he had wanted to be a magician.
19. "I'll show you," said Ed, grinning at Mickey, and Ed asked Mickey to give him a penny.
20. Ed threw the penny on the table and said "Abracadabra," and the penny disappeared.

CHAPTER 17:
CORRECT USE OF VERBS

DIAGNOSTIC TEST, page 15
A.

	ERROR	CORRECT
1.	have raised	have risen
2.	would have lived	had lived
3.	to have cleaned up	to clean up
4.	to discover	to have discovered
5.	are laying	are lying
6.	C	
7.	had turned	turned
8.	C	
9.	had brought	bring
10.	was	were
11.	sit	set
12.	was	were
13.	to remodel	to have remodeled
14.	has lain	has laid
15.	C	

B.

16.	Do want	18.	were	20.	were
17.	agree	19.	should		

POSTTEST, page 16
A.

	ERROR	CORRECT
1.	raised	rose
2.	would have changed	had changed
3.	to have announced	to announce
4.	C	
5.	had driven	drove
6.	was	were
7.	C	
8.	had grown	grow
9.	was failing	were failing
10.	C	
11.	had begun	began
12.	sat	set
13.	would have laid	would have lain
14.	had made	made
15.	would have arrived	had arrived

B.

16. Can explain
17. come
18. wear
19. be
20. were

CHAPTER 18:
CORRECT USE OF MODIFIERS

DIAGNOSTIC TEST, page 17

A.

1. any other
2. sharpest
3. bad
4. easier
5. any other
6. C
7. slowly
8. taller
9. well
10. peacefully
11. better
12. C
13. most accurate
14. well
15. slowly

B.

16. most celebrated
17. regularly
18. most
19. unbelievable
20. competitively

POSTTEST, page 18

A.

1. most recent
2. tightly
3. C
4. enthusiastically
5. more
6. worse
7. well
8. bad
9. heaviest
10. C
11. faster
12. brightest
13. C
14. hardest
15. any other

B.

16. secretly
17. bravely
18. more
19. resourceful
20. honorably

CHAPTER 19:
PLACEMENT OF MODIFERS

DIAGNOSTIC TEST, page 19

A.

(Answers may vary. Possible responses are given.)

1. Danielle made a table with wooden legs for her uncle.
2. Full of pride, Georgio set the main course on the table.
3. Janine took the horse, limping from its injury, to the vet.
4. Tell Jane I would like to meet her after school.
5. Julio was congratulated by the mayor on the proposal.
6. At the auction, Robinson bought some old tools for his father.

7. At the mall, I saw a movie about gorillas.
8. Kiki saw a pair of robins making a nest in the apple tree.
9. I received Marissa's postcard mailed from South America.
10. He gave a tank of tropical fish with vivid colors and shapes to his wife.

B.

(Answers may vary. Possible responses are given.)

11. If you want to visit one of the richest agricultural areas in the United States, take a trip to the Central Valley in California.
12. C
13. While the valley covers a large area north to south, the width of the valley is less than fifty miles.
14. The valley is flanked on the west by the Coast Ranges and on the east by the Sierra Nevada Mountains.
15. In the northern part of the valley, walnut orchards spread over the countryside.
16. Further south, other orchards grow apricots, pears, and peaches.
17. Boxes of tomatoes ready for processing line one farm.
18. Farmers often have to pick fruit before it is ripened.
19. One of the leading crops in Fresno County is grapes.
20. Many of the varieties of grapes cultivated in California are raisin grapes.

POSTTEST, page 20

A.

(Answers may vary. Possible responses are given.)

1. For her grandfather, Elena made a stew with chicken thighs.
2. Without fear, Henry rescued the stranded puppy.
3. The mother lion taught her cub, although still quite young, to hunt .
4. Janine made a bed filled with straw for the kittens.
5. Nina's employer praised her for a job well done.
6. At the sale, I picked up some new CDs for my mother.
7. I could see my keys locked in the car.
8. Orlando saw a large bass leaping out of the water to catch a bug.
9. Tell Tiko to meet me in the lobby before the concert begins.
10. For dinner, Monte made shrimp scampi resting on a bed of noodles.

B.

(Answers may vary. Possible responses are given.)

11. C
12. In the North Cascades Mountains, which are in the state of Washington, twenty-eight smoke jumpers are on call from June to October each year.
13. Grabbing her parachuting gear when the siren sounds, Kasey pulls on her fire-resistant jumpsuit and tall boots.
14. Kasey runs to the small two-engine plane waiting on the runway for clearance.

15. After the plane circles over the fire, Kasey jumps from the plane and pops open her parachute.
16. She and her team members may use chainsaws or explosives for cutting down burning trees.
17. If it is needed, water comes from air-dropped tanks or local sources.
18. While trying to protect the wilderness, smoke jumpers want to put out fires quickly.
19. In 1989, Kasey began smoke-jumper training for eight hours each day.
20. Although the job is dangerous, she loves her work.

CHAPTER 20:
A GLOSSARY OF USAGE

DIAGNOSTIC TEST, page 21
A.

1. as fast as	9. immigrated
2. could have	10. implied
3. nor	11. live
4. number	12. nauseated
5. that	13. notorious
6. from	14. any
7. illusion	15. adapted
8. any	

B.

	ERROR	*CORRECT*
16.	C	
17.	then	than
18.	C	
19.	like	as if
20.	Being as	Because

POSTTEST, page 22
A.

1. adopted	9. be
2. emigrated	10. have
3. somewhat	11. than
4. who	12. alumnae
5. notorious	13. ever
6. allusion	14. as far as
7. nauseous	15. from
8. imply	

B.

	ERROR	*CORRECT*
16.	like	as if
17.	no	any
18.	C	
19.	credulous	credible
20.	amount	number

CHAPTER 21:
CAPITAL LETTERS

DIAGNOSTIC TEST, page 23
A.
1. Great Sphinx; Egypt; Great Pyramid of Cheops
2. Igor Stravinsky; *The Rite of Spring*
3. Why; Ralph's Car Ranch; Church Street
4. "Purple Kite"
5. American Association of Retired Persons; *Modern Maturity*
6. *Charlotte Dundas*; Scotland
7. Inter-American Court of Human Rights; Organization of American States; American Convention on Human Rights
8. Charlotte Brontë; *Jane Eyre*; Emily; *Wuthering Heights*
9. World War I; British; Bertrand Russell
10. Mediterranean Sea; Eagle II
11. Hubert; Sierra Nevada; Rocky Mountains
12. November; Roman Catholic; All Souls' Day; Election Day
13. American; Washington High School
14. Grandmother; Portuguese; Route 21
15. Martin; *Peter Pan*

B.
16. Great Wall of China; Tuesday
17. Yellow Sea
18. Shih Huang Ti
19. *(correct)*
20. China's; Beijing

POSTTEST, page 24
A.
1. Star Market; Walden Pond
2. *Kitchen*; Japanese; Banana Yoshimoto
3. Miami; Miami Dolphins
4. Carnegie Library; December
5. Did; Peabody Fellowship
6. Senator Bob Kerry; Saturday
7. Jupiter
8. *Chicago Sun-Times*
9. The Bookstore in My Mind
10. Roman Catholic; Middle Ages
11. American Nurses Association; Missouri
12. Polaris; North Star; Northern Hemisphere
13. Algebra; Repromax
14. Spanish
15. Colosseum of Rome

B.
16. Minoans; Mycenaeans; Greece
17. The; Minoans; Crete; Mycenaeans; Greek; Iona
18. Greek; Mycenaeans; *Iliad*; *Odyssey*
19. *(correct)*
20. Tiryns; Mycenae; Thebes

CHAPTER 22:
PUNCTUATION

DIAGNOSTIC TEST, page 25
A.
1. Kwok opened the curtain, looked outside, and saw a flock of geese.
2. Lena's home, a blue, two-story house with black shutters, is for sale in Iowa City, Iowa.
3. If you want answers, ask questions.
4. Does Mikhail Baryshnikov, who is one of the world's greatest ballet dancers, still perform?
5. *(correct)*
6. Are we going to go jogging tonight, Toni?

7. The cyclists must ride at least 60 km today, but tomorrow's course is only 20 km.
8. Woven into her braids, the thin, gold ribbon made her hair shine.
9. Please write a note to J. M. Blue, Sr., at P.O. Box 1311, Pigeon Cove, MA 01966.
10. Yikes, does that fish stink!
11. She likes to tell everyone that she served as president from September 7, 1993, to June 5, 1994.
12. Mary asked, "When shall we pick up Hannah for the movie?"

B.

13. As far as the eye could see, the trail traveled a twisting, steep path.
14. Victor, the group leader, suggested that they stop for the night.
15. While setting up camp, they heard a bear.
16. Well, the bear, a scarred, old warrior, kept his distance, but they could still hear him.
17. The hikers, many of whom had met bears before, knew the smart thing to do was to sit by the fire together.
18. Victor reminded everyone not to feed animals in their natural habitat.
19. (*correct*)
20. In the morning the only evidence of the bear was its huge paw prints, which circled the perimeter of the camp.

POSTTEST, page 26

A.

1. The storm, which had developed overnight, blanketed us with 5 ft of snow.
2. Newspapers, recyclable and easy to collect, are picked up every Monday at 9:30 A.M. by the recycling crew.
3. (*correct*)
4. Shall we make stir-fry tonight, Leslie?
5. Did you answer, "Yes"?
6. What a thrilling, suspenseful film that was!
7. Finally, they deciphered the directions and found his house in Santa Fe, New Mexico.
8. Alfred, the youngest of five boys, visited us on July 4, 1994.
9. Tonight we need our rest, for tomorrow promises to be an eventful and trying day.
10. Leo, June, and Nam, all foreign exchange students, shared stories about their exchange families in Bolivia, Japan, and France.
11. Well, that's a lovely idea, but she already has a watch.
12. The comedian told his jokes, bowed to the audience, and walked off the stage.

B.

13. Why, even John Wallace, Jr., who says he hates carrots, loves my dad's morning-glory muffins.
14. On weekend mornings in the kitchen, my dad is busy grating carrots, mixing batter, and popping muffins into the oven.
15. Of course, he experiments now and then.
16. When Alani sent us an enormous, fresh pineapple from Hawaii, my dad added chopped pineapple to the recipe, which made it extra moist.

17. (*correct*)
18. I like to watch from the landing on the stairs.
19. The windows, covered with steam from the hot oven, shimmer with morning light.
20. This wonderful spell is usually broken, however, after John, Jr., smells the muffins and races down the stairs.

CHAPTER 23: PUNCTUATION

DIAGNOSTIC TEST, page 27

A.

1. b.	8. b.
2. b.	9. a.
3. b.	10. b.
4. a.	11. a.
5. b.	12. a.
6. b.	13. a.
7. a.	14. a.

B.

15. "Yes," I answered, "the book's characters are part of New York's high society of the 1870s."
16. I continued, "Wharton also wrote the following novels: The House of Mirth (my favorite), The Custom of the Country, and Ethan Frome; and she wrote short stories, plays, poetry, and travel books as well."
17. Wanda said, "I enjoyed Wharton's short story 'Roman Fever.'"
18. "She was—I'm sure I'm right about this—the first woman to receive the Pulitzer Prize for fiction," I said.
19. Her achievements didn't stop there; she was given an honorary degree from Yale University and in 1930 became a member of the American Academy of Arts and Letters.
20. This woman wasn't only a writer; she received an award for humanitarian work during World War I.

POSTTEST, page 28

A.

1. b.	8. b.
2. a.	9. b.
3. b.	10. b.
4. b.	11. a.
5. a.	12. a.
6. a.	13. b.
7. a.	14. b.

B.

15. "Yes," I replied, "but I don't have the original recipe; therefore, let's use one in the 'Favorite Home-Baked Breads' chapter of Today's Cooking: Fifty Easy-to-Follow Recipes."
16. "Do you have any extra loaf pans I could borrow?" asked Felix.
17. We went to the store and picked up four different types of raisins: seedless raisins, golden raisins, currants, and muscats.
18. In a bowl, I combined the basic ingredients for bread—eggs, scalded milk, butter, flour, and yeast.

19. Then I began squeezing the dough (called
    kneading); consequently, the dough could
    begin to rise.
20. After several hours' wait, we added the most
    delicious ingredients of all, the raisins and
    the walnuts.

CHAPTER 24:
SPELLING

DIAGNOSTIC TEST, page 29
A.

1. bushes
2. immaterial
3. C
4. geese
5. wolves
6. usable
7. proceed
8. reliable
9. paid
10. Kelleys
11. C
12. easily
13. pianos
14. tomatoes
15. passers-by

B.

16. (*correct*)
17. sledding
18. Skating
19. received
20. succeed

A.

1. really
2. supersede
3. Chiefly
4. theories
5. merriment
6. Chomskys
7. waltzes
8. C
9. wolves
10. runners-up
11. C
12. feet
13. C
14. heroes
15. solos

B.

16. sisters-in law
17. unbelievable
18. bagging
19. paid
20. (*correct*)